The Future of
Higher Education

Also available from Continuum

Internationalizing the University, Yvonne Turner and Sue Robson

Pedagogy and the University, Monica McLean

Perspectives of Quality in Adult Learning, Peter Boshier

Reflective Teaching in Further and Adult Education, 2nd Edition, Yvonne Hillier

Rethinking Universities, Sally Baker and Brian J. Brown

Teaching in Further Education 6th Edition, L.B. Curzon

Teaching in Post-Compulsory Education 2nd Edition, Fred Fawbert

The Future of Higher Education

Policy, Pedagogy and the Student Experience

Edited by

Les Bell, Mike Neary and Howard Stevenson

continuum

Continuum International Publishing Group

The Tower Building   80 Maiden Lane,
11 York Road   Suite 704
London SE1 7NX   New York, NY 10038

www.continuumbooks.com

British Library Cataloguing-in-Publication Data
A catalogue record for this book is available from the British Library.

ISBN: 978-1-8470-6472-1 (hardcover)
        978-1-8470-6473-8 (paperback)

Library of Congress Cataloging-in-Publication Data
The future of higher education : policy, pedagogy and the student
experience / edited by Mike Neary, Howard Stevenson and Les Bell.
      p. cm.   Includes bibliographical references and index.
   ISBN 978-1-8470-6473-8 (pb)
   ISBN 978-1-8470-6472-1 (hb)
1. Education, Higher – Aims and objectives – Great Britain. 2. Higher
education and state – Great Britain. 3. Education, Higher – Economic
aspects – Great Britain. 4. Educational change – Great Britain. I. Neary,
Mike, 1956– II. Stevenson, Howard, 1963– III. Bell, Les, 1942– IV. Title.

LA637.F86 2009
378.41–dc22   2008039234

Typeset by Newgen Imaging Systems Pvt Ltd, Chennai, India
Printed and bound in Great Britain by CPI Antony Rowe, Chippenham, Wiltshire

Contents

Preface

The purpose of this book is to explore policy, pedagogy and the student experience in higher education at a conceptual level, enabling university staff to place their own work within a wider theoretical framework and to develop their own understandings of some of the key controversies that surround teaching and learning in higher education. The introduction explores significant policy developments that have shaped the learning landscape of higher education. The book is then divided into three parts, the first of which analyses key issues in higher education: academic freedom, sustainability and the nature of the learning landscape and traces the impact that these policies have had on the extent and nature of higher education provision. The second part demonstrates how these emerging policies, and the need for higher education institutions to respond to them, have produced a radical re-evaluation of what higher education is and how it might best be delivered at an institutional level. The final part gives consideration to pedagogy and the student experience in contemporary higher education, focusing on the experiences of mature students, student involvement in quality assurance and the student as producer.

This book is written by the staff of the Centre for Educational Research and Development (CERD) at the University of Lincoln. CERD is a new organization, formed in 2007 by the amalgamation of the Teaching and Learning Development Office (TLDO) and the International Institute for Educational Leadership (IIEL). The TLDO was generally responsible for quality enhancement and the implementation of the University's Teaching and Learning Strategy, including running professional development programmes for staff, administering the Teacher Fellow programme, and promoting the effective use of educational technology and virtual learning environments. IIEL provided masters and doctoral level programmes and conducted research in educational leadership. The CERD remit combines an emphasis on learning, teaching and research with the provision of higher degree programmes, focusing on the development of teaching and learning in higher education. Its approach is both academic and scholarly, aiming for the highest standards of academic professional practice through an application of the scholarship of teaching and learning. Although grounded in the academic tradition, CERD is committed to experimentation and innovation in teaching and learning; the basic pedagogic principles for the Centre's research and development activities are derived from the most progressive and critical pedagogies applied to the contemporary teaching and learning situation. Although focused on teaching and learning in higher education, CERD is engaged with other areas of formal and informal educational provision. In the formal sector this includes working with schools and colleges; in the informal, working with the community and voluntary sector on the delivery of education programmes.

In producing this volume we have been ably support by our administrative colleagues Jill Hubbard and Beverley Potterton. We are grateful for the help and encouragement of Kirsty Schaper, Jo Allcock and all the staff at Continuum Books. We all owe a considerable debt of gratitude to Penny Brown of Good Impressions Academic Editing (**www.good-impressions.net**) for her insightful suggestions and thorough editing of the final manuscript.

Les Bell
Mike Neary
Howard Stevenson
University of Lincoln, August 2008

Notes on Contributors

Julian Beckton is Teaching and Learning Co-ordinator. Before moving into the field of Educational Development he worked in academic libraries for a number of years. Julian has been involved in a number of projects including the integration of personal development planning into university curricula, the development and support of Virtual Learning Environments and the introduction of plagiarism management software. He is currently working on setting up a Learning Object Repository.

Les Bell is Professor of Educational Leadership at the University of Lincoln and Emeritus Professor of Educational Management at the University of Leicester. He taught in both primary and secondary schools before joining the Education Department at Coventry College of Education. He subsequently became a member of the Education Department at the University of Warwick after the two institutions merged. In 1994 Les became Director of the School of Education and Community Studies at Liverpool John Moores University and was appointed to the Chair of Educational Management at Leicester in 1999. He has written extensively on educational management and leadership; his latest book, *Perspectives on Educational Management and Leadership* (2007) is published by Continuum.

Karin Crawford is a Principal Teaching Fellow. Her research interests and publications include both pedagogy and Health and Social Care. Karin is principally interested in using qualitative, narrative approaches to further the understanding of lifelong learning and academic practice. She has written several books and articles on professional development and improving teaching and training in higher education. Her book *Practice Education in Social Work: A Handbook for Practice Teachers, Assessors and Educators* was co-authored with Janet Walker and Jonathan Parker, and was published by Learning Matters, Exeter, in 2008.

Andy Hagyard joined the University of Lincoln in 1995 and for the last seven years has worked as a Learning and Teaching Co-ordinator. Part of this role is running institutional student satisfaction surveys; he is a member of the Higher Education Academy working group which explores effective use of National Student Survey data. He represents the University as a member of the LearnHigher Centre for Excellence in Teaching and Learning, and is on the steering group of the new Association for Learning Development in Higher Education.

Terence Karran is Senior Academic and Docent Professor at the University of Oulu, Finland and the former Chair of the Board of the Euro Study Centres of the European Association of Distance Teaching Universities. From 2005 to 2007 he was Visiting Professor at the Autonomous University of Guadalajara in Mexico, where he was the Director of the Distance Learning Centre and of the Mexican National Co-ordination Centre for the World Bank Institute's Global Development Learning Network for Latin America and the Caribbean. He has written extensively on teaching and learning in higher education.

Pam Locker is a Principal Teaching Fellow. She entered full time teaching following a successful career as a Museum and Exhibition Designer. She has been a member of collaborative teams for a number of educational environments and produced a series of films aimed at teaching drawing skills to design students. Pam's research interests are in the educational nature of communicative environments as a vehicle for understanding complicated ideas, the use of interactive media in the promotion and education of health issues in young people, and the function and use of the Blended Studio in design pedagogy for undergraduate design students.

Aileen Morris began teaching in further education in 1984. She joined De Montfort University in 1997, where she both supported undergraduate and postgraduate students in the research, planning and production of degree work and delivered the PGCE and CertEd. Since 2003 she has managed and delivered the PGCE in Post Compulsory Learning and Teaching programme (now the PGDE in Higher Education Teaching and Learning) at the University of Lincoln. Aileen is currently reading for a Doctorate in Education at the University of Sheffield. Her particular research interests are in the higher education learning experiences of students from under-represented groups and teacher identity in higher education.

Mike Neary is Professor and Dean of Teaching and Learning, and the Director of the Centre for Educational Research and Development. Mike was the founding director of the Reinvention Centre for Undergraduate Research, a Centre for Excellence based at Warwick and Oxford Brookes Universities, the aim of which is to introduce research-based learning into the undergraduate curriculum. Mike combines his teaching and research activities through writing about his own teaching practice in the context of national and international educational policy. He has been an adviser and consultant for the Higher Education Academy Subject Centre Network, is a National Teaching Fellow and has written extensively on teaching and learning in higher education.

Terfot Ngwana is a Senior Lecturer in Education. His interest in education for sustainable development is derived from his background in international education and development. For the last seven years he has been involved in research in both teaching and learning and higher education. His current research interests include the internationalization of the higher education curriculum, sustainability in higher education teaching and learning and the international trade in higher education services.

Angela Thody is Emeritus Professor of Education. She joined the University as a professor in 1996, having previously held posts at Leicester, Luton, De Montfort and the Open University. She specializes in methods of research writing and lecturing and in education leadership. In these fields, she has written five books, edited and contributed to five books, and authored over 50 articles in professional and academic journals as well as numerous chapters and research reports. Angela edited a journal of the British Education Leadership Management and Administration Society for seven years and was President of the Commonwealth Council for Educational Administration for six years.

Howard Stevenson taught in secondary schools for 15 years before becoming Senior Lecturer at the University of Leicester and Deputy Director of the Centre for Educational Leadership and Management. He is now Deputy Director of the Centre for Educational Research and Development. His research and publishing interests relate to the development and formulation of educational policy processes in both schools and post-compulsory education. He is the author, with Professor Les Bell, of *Education Policy: Process, themes and outcomes* (Routledge, 2006).

Sue Watling joined the University of Lincoln's widening participation team, Educational Partnerships, where she created a virtual campus to support links between the University of Lincoln and its partner schools and colleges. In her present post Sue provides support to staff constructing online learning areas and content, with emphasis on quality assurance for distance and flexible learning and compliance with current accessibility legislation. Her interests include developing opportunities for online interaction and formative self assessment through reusable learning objects. She is currently researching the student experience of elearning.

Joss Winn is Technology Support Officer. He is currently working to establish the University's Open Access Institutional Repository of peer-reviewed research and teaching and learning objects. Besides Open Access to research, he has a continuing interest in Open Source software development and the Free Culture movement. Joss has an MA in Film Archiving from the University of East Anglia and an MA in Buddhist Studies from the University of Michigan. He previously worked at Amnesty International and the BFI National Film and Television Archive.

Introduction – Universities in Transition: Themes in Higher Education Policy

Howard Stevenson and Les Bell

Introduction: higher education – the policy arena and the learning landscape

This book is about the ways in which policy changes in the structure, governance, funding and provision of higher education are reshaping the learning landscape of higher education. The term 'learning landscape' includes the physical architecture, the formal and informal relationships, the processes of teaching, learning and assessment, the deployment of technology and the other factors that combine to shape the nature of the student experience in higher education. The book does not set out to explore in detail the changes in educational policy to which higher education has been subjected since the middle of the twentieth century, nor does it concern itself with the detail of university administration. These matters have been covered extensively in many other volumes (e.g. Warner and Palfreyman 2001; Barnett 2005a). This first chapter will, however, trace briefly the main policy themes that are of particular significance to the focus of this book. These include the consensus about university autonomy that exemplified policy until the 1960s, the merging of the public and private sectors of higher education, the widening of participation, the impact of changes in university funding and the increasing emphasis on the economic role of universities today, and the changing nature of the learning landscape in higher education.

The development of education policy can best be understood as a contested process in which those with competing values and differential access to power seek to form and shape policy in their own interests. The notion of policy as the pursuit of fundamentally political objectives is recognized in Kogan's seminal study of educational policy-making, in which he defines policies as the 'operational statements of values' and the 'authoritative allocation of values' (Kogan 1975: 55). This helpfully locates policy within a context of wider fundamental questions: what is education for? who is education for? who decides and on what basis? As subsequent chapters in this book will show, debates about these issues continue to influence higher education policy to the present day, revealing conflicting sets of values and different views about the very nature and purpose of higher education.

Kogan (1975) places the identification of competing values at the centre of understanding the development of higher education policy in the United Kingdom. Similarly recognizing the importance of values in shaping educational policy, Collier (1982) identified four central values that, he argued, underpin and inform educational policy. These are:

- academic – academic freedom, professional autonomy, concern for academic disciplines, conceptual clarification and precision, and the intrinsic value of education;
- egalitarianism – social justice, equality of opportunity and access, social mobility, personal autonomy;
- economic renewal – provision of trained labour force, contribution to economic well-being, increasing productivity, market forces;
- consensus – resolving disputes by accommodation, a minimum of public confrontation.

To these might be added:

- institutional values – freedom from state control, participation, institutional maintenance (Kogan 1975).

At the same time, social justice might be elevated to a significant set of values in its own right while, from the late 1980s onwards, the values of the market-place combine with the human capital elements of economic renewal to exert considerable influence over higher education policy (Bell and Stevenson 2006).

The development of policy in the university sector in the United Kingdom is typified by conflict between competing values, especially between academic values and the increasing demand that universities should contribute directly to economic renewal and maintenance, as subsequent chapters will show. Nevertheless, this identification of a competing range of values, such as those listed above, is helpful to the extent that it can shed light on the relative importance of the different factors that drive policy, while recognizing that those policies may themselves be identified by more than one value. For example, the gradual expansion of university provision during the immediate post-war period was, in a period characterized largely by cross-party consensus and a commitment to the expansion of educational provision, defended on educational, economic and social grounds:

> Social and economic values thus dominated the original educational and institutional assumptions. In 1950, the universities were untouchable because it was assumed that they should best be allowed to have their own ideals of excellence and their own ways to contribute to the social good. This would be enough accountability. (Kogan 1975: 198)

Becher and Kogan (1983) note that values operate at different levels: governmental, institutional, departmental and individual. The relative importance of different sets of values and their concomitant policy processes and outcomes may be contested at each of these levels, although the dominant values in the socio-political environment at any particular time are most likely to shape the discourse that informs policy formulation and implementation (Bell and Stevenson 2006). This discourse will pervade higher education and shape policies that, in turn, influence its organization and operation.

In recent years all aspects of education in the United Kingdom and in many other countries have been subject to significant changes resulting from the policies of the respective national governments. These policies are often contentious and contested. However, it was only at the start of the last quarter of the twentieth century that the prospect of these disputes was beginning to emerge:

> Education is not a zone of public policy in which dramatic events are expected. It is not at the centre of the national policy stage, though in the last ten years it has become an area of controversy and interest. (Kogan 1975: 227)

This lack of dramatic policy shifts in education was primarily because in the immediate post-war period education policy had been largely concerned with resourcing and consolidating provision.

The learning landscape of higher education began to change significantly in the late 1940s, as more universities were created. Exeter, Keele, Leicester, Nottingham and Southampton all received charters (Kogan 1975). These changes were driven by the need to cope with the growing pressure for university places. This was a period of gradual growth and development as yet untouched by the ideologies of expansion, human capital or mass higher education. Universities were still relatively autonomous and elitist institutions which were intent on offering to their graduates 'the breadth of outlook necessary for those who are to fill positions of responsibility . . . [and] . . . the chance to become . . . capable and cultivated human beings' (Kogan 1975: 194). Academic values predominated, although those values were later to be fiercely contested.

The Robbins Report: an era of expansion

By the end of the 1950s it became clear that gradual expansion was not going to yield the growth that was required, largely because universities raised their entry requirements to cope with increased demand, rather than accommodating larger groups of students within the existing infrastructure. This resulted in the establishment of the Committee on Higher Education to inquire into the future development of the sector. Its report, commonly referred to as the Robbins Report after its chairman Lord Robbins, was published in 1963. This report stated that 'all young persons qualified by ability and attainment to pursue a full-time course in higher education should have the opportunity to do so' (Committee on Higher Education 1963: 49). This reflection provided a guide for the development of the British higher education system thereafter. The subsequent expansion was pioneered by the Open University which, within three years of its foundation in 1969, had 40,000 part-time undergraduate students – these were mainly mature, part-time students who had jobs and often family commitments and who were being given the opportunity to obtain a degree via a credit/module system through distance learning. The popularity of the Open University and its rate of success seriously challenged the idea, formerly widespread, that there was a limited pool of ability in any country. The Robbins Report also led to the establishment of the so-called plate glass universities, notably the universities of East Anglia, Kent, Lancaster, Stirling, Sussex, York and Warwick (Beloff 1968). Despite the recommendations of the Robbins Committee, this further expansion of higher education mainly took place in the non-university sector of higher and further education.

The non-university sector of further and higher education, almost entirely under local authority control, was emerging as a powerful force in competition with universities. By the mid-1970s there were 30 university-status polytechnics offering degrees which were validated by the Council for National Academic Awards (CNAA). They were seen as 'providing a network of educational provision for any citizen who cares to avail himself of it from the age of sixteen to retirement' (Kogan 1975: 186). These polytechnics, many of them emerging from technical colleges and already as big as average sized universities, were based on a tradition of public provision and service and were concerned with the practical application of knowledge while, at the same time, espousing the scholarly values associated with universities. However, 'the polytechnics, so eager to demonstrate the superiority of public purpose over elitism, soon acquired characteristics remarkably similar to those of the universities' (Kogan 1975: 216), and so it proved as educational policy developed over the next three decades. Although powerful voices questioned the wisdom of maintaining separate sectors of higher education (Fowler 1983) the binary system lasted until 1992, when the polytechnics were granted university status. In 1992 the Further and Higher Education Act (Office of Public Sector Information 1992) dissolved both the Universities Funding Council and the Polytechnics and Colleges Funding Council and established a Higher Education Funding Council. Polytechnics were given university status (and are now usually described as 'post-1992' or 'new' universities while those institutions with university status prior to that date are termed 'pre-1992 universities').

Although these policy developments in both the university and polytechnic sectors were still largely structural and justified mainly on social or egalitarian grounds, economists such as Vaizey argued that education should be seen as an investment, while the expansionist education policies of the then Secretary of State for Education, David Eccles, were being justified on the grounds of providing competitive advantage in world markets (Kogan 1975). Nevertheless, there were alternative views:

> The economy and manpower values are in variable relationship with egalitarianism and personal freedom. For example, in the expansion of higher education, society simultaneously provides for the improvement of the economy and the trained manpower to service it, for opportunities for personal development and freedom, for the creation of an elite, and for a more equal society. There is no automatic argument justifying all the places in higher education on the grounds of productivity. (Kogan 1975: 64)

The Robbins Committee appeared to establish social demand as the firm imperative guiding admission to higher education. In a major part of the report, however, it was argued that expansion was based primarily on human capital rather than egalitarian or social justice considerations. The development and diffusion of skills was a primary objective in higher education, especially in view of a growing need to maintain competitive advantage: 'The communities that have paid most attention to higher studies have in general been the most obviously progressive in respect of income and wealth' (Committee on Higher Education 1963: 206). Interestingly, however, although the Committee approvingly quoted the classical economists, it did not develop the argument of these same writers that where an educational institution is made more dependent for its funds on fees paid directly out of the customers' pocket, more competition between suppliers will result (West 1963).

In the two decades following the Robbins-driven expansion, higher education experienced turbulent times as demand for places declined, economic growth wavered and the oil crisis shook national confidence (Bell 2007). It became clear that there were two distinctly different views about the purposes of universities and the nature of the concomitant learning landscapes required to achieve these purposes. On the one hand was the idealistic view of the self-motivated, self-regulated community of disinterested scholars, teaching and researching without external direction or control. The scholars' primary motivation was to further their subjects and to hold the intellectual high ground. At the other extreme was the utilitarian view of justification by measurable results, or output, in terms of trained and compliant employees. Here scholars were seen as researching and teaching for the material betterment of society as judged by their paymasters. The scholars' responsibility was to society, or to the national economy, rather than to their subjects (Broers 2005).

In the pursuance of the currently predominant utilitarian perspective, it is argued that higher education is now subject to two complementary forces: mercantilism and dirigisme (Gombrich 2000). The former is based on the belief that free markets and economic priorities should determine policy, while the latter involves the continued increase of state intervention in the structure and funding of higher education institutions. State control over both funding and the work of universities did increase, justified on the grounds that universities needed to make a more effective contribution to national economic development (Gombrich 2000). Assessment of both research (through the Research Assessment Exercise) and teaching (through the work of the Quality Assurance Agency for Higher Education) was introduced, giving rise to what has been termed the 'Faustian compact' between universities and state that has established, in exchange for state funding, an elaborate process of scrutiny, evaluation, measurement and quality assurance (Broers 2005). As was seen above, by 1992 the binary system was, to all intents and purposes, abolished. Such changes were clearly significant and far-reaching. Nevertheless, the period between 1992 and 1997 was characterized by retrenchment in both the statutory and post-compulsory sectors, most graphically illustrated in higher education by a cap on undergraduate recruitment and significant reductions in unit cost per student spending in the sector.

The Dearing Report: higher education and the global economy

The election of New Labour in 1997 marked a key and decisive shift in British politics (Bell and Stevenson 2006; Bell 2007). While the new administration clearly sought to work within the parameters of the neo-liberal agenda, it was also clear that New Labour had no intention of reproducing Thatcherism's crude repudiation of the state. In fact, education was regarded by New Labour as having a key role in sustaining the state both socially, by inculcating notions of citizenship, and economically, by providing a skilled labour force. Given the party's social democratic tradition, it was always likely that values of social justice and citizenship would have a conspicuous role in shaping education policy, in spite of the human capital overtones of many of the policy statements (Bell and Stevenson 2006). These diverse values produced a series of tensions within education policy, especially as it related to higher education. This tension in policy was immediately exposed by the Labour government's commitment to expand the higher education sector, but to achieve this by introducing student fees for tuition costs. Expansion was in part advanced as an equity argument, and an emerging discourse related to widening participation has since developed. However, the case for expansion was also an economic one, based on the need to increase the nation's skills base. At the same time the decision to introduce student fees revealed further policy tensions. Critics have argued that fees disproportionately deter those from low income backgrounds who are likely to be more debt-averse and that this would mitigate against widening participation. It is further argued that fees undermine the universalist principle of the welfare state and transform the student into little more than a consumer in the market-place. In contrast, there is an argument that universal welfarism was never genuinely equitable and simply represented a regressive redistribution of income as working class tax payers funded middle class access to the universities.

The new government responded to these complex issues by commissioning Sir Ron Dearing to present a 20-year vision for the development of higher education. Although not on the scale or significance of the Robbins Report, the National Committee of Inquiry into Higher Education (NCIHE) report, usually termed the Dearing Report (NCIHE 1997), nevertheless performed a similar function. The intention was to frame the discourse shaping higher education policy and the learning landscape, and thereby set the parameters within which higher education policy would be developed in the coming years. The outcome was neither groundbreaking nor dramatic, but it did signal a clear reversal of the policy of retrenchment that had characterized the recent past. Dearing's report highlighted the central contribution that higher education could and should make to the collective quality of life in the twenty-first century – economically, socially and culturally. It identified the following aims:

- to enable individuals to develop their capabilities to the highest potential levels throughout life, so that they grow intellectually, are well equipped for work, can contribute effectively to society and achieve personal fulfilment;
- to increase knowledge and understanding for their own sake and foster their application for the benefit of the economy and society;
- to serve the needs of an adaptable, sustainable, knowledge-based economy at local, regional and national levels;
- to play a major role in shaping a democratic, civilized, inclusive society (after NCIHE 1997).

In many respects the Dearing Report acknowledged the traditional role of the university, which it defined as contributing to the intellectual development of students, equipping them for work, adding to the world's store of knowledge and understanding and fostering culture for its own sake (NCIHE 1997). However, it also signalled a shift in emphasis within higher education by recognizing its pivotal role in contributing to commercial success in a globalized economy. Within Dearing's analysis it is possible to identify a number of key issues that have subsequently, and decisively, shaped the development of higher education policy. Three issues in particular have driven recent policy in the higher education sector, and these are likely to have a continuing influence on shaping the landscape on which higher education policy is developed. First is a particular analysis of the world economy as knowledge-driven and global. Second is a policy response that sees competitive advantage secured through the development of human capital. Third is a view that the state has a facilitating role in securing these objectives, but that market forces drive innovation and provide value for money in the public sector. Each of these issues is explored in turn, and the implications for the recent and future development of higher education policy are identified.

The economies of the advanced capitalist countries face significant challenges as a consequence of globalization. Relatively high labour costs and the increased mobility of capital have resulted in the virtual demise of the manufacturing base in these countries, as the lower cost economies of Asia and the new Europe have become the factories of the world. While capital may welcome the emergence of a global economy without borders, the governments of nation states must juggle the pressure to promote free trade with the need to protect their own citizens from the negative consequences of a strident neo-liberalism. Social theorists in these economies (Drucker 1969; Bell 1973) have sought succour in the concept of the knowledge economy – a belief that competitive advantage is secured by high value-added through innovation, technological development and creativity, and that the source of such advantage is knowledge. According to this analysis, knowledge generation, processing and transmission become the key factor of production (Castells 2000), superseding land, labour and capital as the fundamental sources of productivity and power (Guile 2006).

Within this scenario universities have a key role to play. If knowledge is the source of competitive advantage then universities, as the sites of knowledge production, become pivotal to economic success:

> Research and development are seen as crucial because by capturing intellectual property rights (IPR) companies gain a monopoly that gives them an advantage over their rivals. In effect they are seen as the primary source of wealth in the knowledge economy. But, of course, making the intellectual breakthroughs that lead to property rights requires top-class research and development, much of which resides in universities. (Lauder et al. 2006: 33)

However, universities are not concerned purely with the production of knowledge, but increasingly with its exchange and trade. In such circumstances knowledge itself becomes commodified, the subject of a market transaction, with a value determined by its perceived contribution to potential capital accumulation or future earnings. Moreover, this is a global market-place in which knowledge producers and knowledge consumers (whether commercial organizations purchasing IPRs or individual students securing qualifications) bargain over output. This is a process which increasingly operates across national borders.

Belief in knowledge as the source of competitive advantage reinforces the view that the route to economic success is through investment in human capital. If economies in the advanced capitalist nations can only compete to a limited extent – by driving down wages and de-regulating labour markets – then productivity must be secured through increased output and high value-added. This is the business case for investment in education and training. It is the rationale for the substantial expansion of the higher education sector and is clearly articulated in a report by Lord Leitch:

> For developed countries that cannot compete on natural resources and low labour costs, success demands a more service-led economy and high value-added industry. In the 21st Century, our natural resource is our people – and their potential is both untapped and vast. Skills are the key to unlocking that potential. The prize for our country will be enormous – higher productivity, the creation of wealth and social justice. Without increased skills, we would condemn ourselves to a lingering decline in competitiveness, diminishing economic growth and a bleaker future for all . . . Becoming a world leader on skills will enable the UK to compete with the best in the world. (Leitch 2006: 1)

If there is a need to develop knowledge as a source of competitive advantage in the global economy, with a commitment to achieving this through investment in human capital, then potential contradictions in state policy begin to emerge. At one and the same time economic success apparently depends on a substantial investment in education as a public good, while simultaneously global economic constraints limit the ability of national governments to generate revenue from progressive taxation. The response lies in a reconfigured state in which strategic state direction and regulation remain important, but are increasingly complemented by private sector provision and the shift to a 'consumer pays' approach to education policy. While the state has taken an increasingly dominant role in framing the environment in which higher education institutions function, universities are also encouraged to be autonomous and freestanding in a competitive and entrepreneurial market-place. Universities are under increasing pressure to fund their own expansion, whether by private sector funding for research, payment for traded consultancy services or income derived from student fees.

Beyond Dearing – the legislative response

These, then, are the discourses that have shaped higher education policy and the learning landscape in recent years, and which have been reflected in parallel developments across the world. Within the United Kingdom they have underpinned the Higher Education Act (2004), perhaps the most significant policy development in higher education in recent years. It locates higher education firmly within the drive for competitive success in a globalized economy. At the core of the agenda is the continued expansion of the sector and the conviction that training more people at all levels represents the investment in human capital considered necessary for increasing prosperity. The bulk of this expansion is to come through new types of qualification, better tailored to the needs of students and the economy, such as the further development of two-year work-focused foundation degrees (DfES 2003). While it is envisaged that expansion will occur across the sector, the development of more work-related routes to higher education, and in particular the expansion of foundation degrees, suggests that a disproportionate element of this growth will be concentrated in the post-1992 universities, and that the divide between these institutions and the further education sector will become blurred. Such developments have far-reaching implications for the relationships between students and tutors and the continued professional development of staff in universities, as subsequent chapters will show.

In contrast to this general focus on teaching and learning, there is a clear expectation that more research activity – high level knowledge production – will be focused in fewer universities. The report *The Future of Higher Education* (DfES 2003) claims that there is need to reap the benefits which flow from concentrating the best research in larger units and that future investment will focus more on the leading research departments and universities, enabling them to compete with the world's best. There is also a growing expectation among universities that research income will be drawn increasingly from the private sector. Within the so-called non-research intensive universities, the emphasis is on facilitating knowledge exchange rather than production, in particular through the developments of networks and partnerships with local and regional industry.

The corollary of this emerging policy environment is that there will be two interdependent developments across the sector. First is a further increase in institutional hierarchies determined primarily by the distinction between research-based and teaching-based institutions. In many ways this is essentially a distinction between knowledge producers and knowledge transmitters. The traditional university mission has esteemed both these activities (although this is not to argue that they have been esteemed equally). In the current climate it is possible to see knowledge production focused in fewer and fewer institutions, while non-research based institutions deliver the mass qualification system required by Leitch (2006). Hence, the fundamental nature and purpose of universities is undergoing substantial change and institutions of higher education are becoming more diverse in terms both of their mission and their internal characteristics (Barnett 2005a). The very shape of universities is changing:

> They move; their shape changes as . . . their disciplinary base shifts or their interventions with the wider society take on new forms . . . It is as if the university is infinitely extendable; space, it seems, can always be found for new activities, for new agendas and even new discourses. (Barnett 2005a: 2–3)

This changing nature of universities and of university education is reflected further in a learning landscape which incorporates new agencies such as the Higher Education Academy, an increased emphasis on professional development, new structural forms such as Education Development Units (EDUs) and the stretched academy, extended forms of quality assurance that focus on student feedback and the impact of technology on teaching and learning.

The second development is an accelerated process of marketization across the sector. Here there are two specific aspects. First is the need for universities to compete – and therefore to behave as if they were commercial organizations in a market environment. Whether it be competing for students or for research income, universities are increasingly likely to adopt business methods and strategies that appear to secure success in the market. In particular they are likely to develop specialist areas of strength while simultaneously downscaling or closing poorly- performing areas of provision that fail to generate adequate income. Second is a process of integration *into* the market, in which the missions of universities become inseparable from the goals and objectives of the wider economy. This is largely achieved by linking income generation to market-driven imperatives. In research terms, universities must look increasingly to the private sector for research income.

Universities are forced to chase this potential income or lose out on valuable research funding. In this way the research objectives of the university sector are increasingly driven by the business demands of the corporate sector – a phenomenon described by Slaughter and Leslie (1997) as 'academic capitalism'.

The strategic development of the learning landscape and especially of teaching programmes within universities is driven by the same logic. When students pay an increasing proportion of the tuition fees for their courses, with a concomitant impact on their personal debt accumulation, it follows that individual students will take calculated decisions about possible courses and their future earning potential. Courses that offer a route to apparently high-paying occupations are likely to experience increases in demand as the higher potential salary improves the rate of return on the investment in course fees. In this way, courses that link most directly to areas of high demand in the economy are likely to benefit from increased student applications. Similarly, fee-paying students are more likely to adopt the stance of consumers towards their higher education rather than accepting it as intrinsically good in its own right. This in turn is likely to impact on student expectations as the implied contract between provider and consumer focuses on factors such as teaching quality, class size and wider issues of general resourcing. Furthermore, as participation widens and students are recruited from groups traditionally underrepresented in higher education, teaching strategies, learning styles and modes of assessment will need to be reconsidered. Institutional responses to such issues will influence student recruitment and retention. As with research income, business logic dictates that universities expand areas where student demand is high – and contract in areas where demand is low. The consequence of these policy developments is a re-assertion of economic values within the university enterprise. In this new policy environment universities' strategic direction is increasingly driven by the impulses of the wider market economy, while wider social and professional values assume a second order role.

Conclusion: universities in a changing landscape

It can be seen, then, that the learning landscape of higher education has been in almost constant transition since the middle of the twentieth century. Universities have moved from being autonomous, exclusive and largely elitist institutions to potential instruments for social mobility through mass participation. They have developed from isolated seats of esoteric learning to utilitarian contributors to the nation's economic survival. However, shifts in policy do not go uncontested. Policy development is best understood as the outcome of a struggle over values, with conflicts and compromises taking place in different forms, at different times and at different levels of the policy process. From such struggles emerge key themes, which have shaped the contributions to this book. These include the debate about the nature of university education and the degree to which universities can have a role to play in fostering economic advantage; the extent to which academic freedom is compromised by current policy development; and the impact of widening student participation and of technological developments on teaching, learning, the student experience and indeed on the very nature of programmes offered by universities.

It remains the case that the way these developments affect the lived experiences of those who study and work in universities depends crucially on how policy is played out within individual institutions. At this point, for example, the educational values and commitment to social justice of practitioners can emerge, and begin to challenge the market values that underpin the wider system . The impact of individual agency in these circumstances should not be overstated, but its potential importance must be recognized. The actions of practitioners have a crucial role in shaping the learning landscape, the experience of those who study and of others who work in universities. The contributions to this volume begin to set out how this may happen. All the contributors are practitioners in higher education with considerable experience in the field. Each will identify many of the key challenges facing the higher education sector and the consequences for the student experience. Each illustrates the creative ways in which practitioners can reflect on their own practice, locate it within the wider policy environment and develop teaching strategies that reassert the primacy of the learner at the heart of the higher education experience.

Part One
The Policy Context

In the Introduction Bell and Stevenson set out the broad policy context in which higher education functions and which has shaped its learning landscape. Part One of this book explores the policy context in greater detail, acknowledging that higher education is influenced by a globalized world where knowledge itself is claimed to be the source of competitive advantage, while knowledge production and knowledge transmission are presented as pivotal to future prosperity. Universities have become central to this knowledge economy, not purely as sites of knowledge production but because the ideas spawned within them significantly shape the discourses and ideologies that frame the world in which we live. Moreover, while the pressures to produce, transmit and trade certain types of knowledge are necessarily powerful, these pressures are not uncontested. Universities are not factories producing truths, but places where learning landscapes are created and re-created and ideas are developed, critically analysed and challenged. While powerful forces may seek to mould the nature of the work that takes place in academia there remain important opportunities for universities to shape and re-shape the discourses that influence our world. In this section contributors engage with some of the significant issues that emerge from those discourses and the nature of the learning landscapes that develop from them.

Karran confronts directly the issues relating to knowledge production, and the opportunity for those who work in universities to determine the nature of what is produced and transmitted. He argues that academic freedom is not only at the heart of the university mission, but that it is a cornerstone of a democratic society. Despite an almost universal commitment to academic freedom, at least at a rhetorical level, Karran points out that the complex nature of the concept can make it problematic to secure in practice. Academic freedom is about much more than free speech – a concept with which it is often confused. It extends to wider questions of academic study: what is taught and researched, and who decides? In a neo-liberal economic order, where commercial imperatives are so dominant, threats to academic freedom become both more powerful and more complex.

If Karran raises important questions about the nature of academia as work, then Neary and Thody begin to pose similarly fundamental questions about the spaces in which academic work takes place. They explore a concept that is at the core of this volume, that of the learning landscape, and identify how discourses relating to design, architecture and pedagogy are not value-free, but are influential in framing the nature of the academic work that takes place in universities. Most significantly, the learning landscape represents the terrain on which learning takes place and is a key factor in shaping the nature of the relationship between teacher and student. The authors draw on developments such as those at the Reinvention Centre at Warwick University to demonstrate how a creative attitude to space can begin to redefine the nature of the teacher–student relationship in new and radical ways.

Finally, Ngwana demonstrates the complex interplay between universities as institutions and the wider policy environment. Universities have been instrumental in developing an understanding of both global degradation and the steps necessary to promote sustainability. However, as Ngwana argues, universities must go beyond this and develop pedagogical practices that embed notions of sustainability in the curriculum through enhancing sustainability literacy and which can challenge the dissonance that surrounds this topic. His contribution emphasizes that the university curriculum must be both grounded in a sound theoretical understanding of learning and teaching and be coherent and broadly defined in order to ensure that sustainability and sustainable development are not neutral constructs, but a reflection of wider values and priorities in society. In areas such as education for sustainable development, universities must not simply react to, but actively shape a progressive agenda.

Academic Freedom: Essential Liberty or Extravagant Luxury?

Terence Karran

Introduction

Academic freedom is acknowledged as vital to the proper functioning of universities. For example, Nelson (1990: 21) argues that 'academic freedom is the most significant concept a teacher can embrace. The freedom to study, learn, teach and express ideas is the defining characteristic of the concept of academic freedom for teachers and students'. In Europe, such sentiments underpin the European Universities Association's 1988 *Magna Charta Universitatum* which states: 'Freedom in research and training is the fundamental principle of university life, and governments and universities, each as far as in them lies, must ensure respect for this fundamental requirement' (EUA 1988). However, freedom, in various (philosophical, economic, political) guises, has always been a problematic concept within human society. Wars have been fought to remove, restore or protect basic human freedoms; their importance has been explicitly recognized by their inclusion in national constitutions, and supra-national codes like the United Nations' Universal Declaration of Human Rights. Consequently, the granting of an explicit freedom to a particular professional group, which is denied to all other groups in society, is particularly contentious. Moreover, it is not just the granting of this freedom, but the uses to which it has been put which have led to continuing calls for its removal. In past struggles for freedom of speech, university academics were often prominent, because their specialist knowledge enabled them to mount valid attacks on dictatorial governments, monarchies and the church. For example, in 1633 the astronomer Galileo Galilei was imprisoned by the Pope for expressing the belief that the earth moved around the sun, thus contradicting prevailing theological doctrine. Despite the Church's acceptance of the Galilean model of the solar system, tensions still exist between Church and state. Hence, in 2008 Pope Benedict XVI was forced to cancel a visit to La Sapienza University in Rome after lecturers and students protested against a speech in which he opined the Church's verdict against Galileo had been 'rational and just'.

As Thorens has shown 'the historical origin of university autonomy and academic freedom goes back to the High Middle Ages in Europe' (Thorens 2006: 92) when the first universities, in cities such as Bologna, Paris and Oxford, struggled to escape persecution for asserting their rights of self governance and the pursuit of scholarship and teaching without censure or constraint. Consequently, as Traver describes, actions like the Great Dispersion of 1229 which resulted in a migration of staff and students from Paris to Angers, Orleans and Oxford, led to scholarly liberty being 'acknowledged as a university right . . . in 1231, in Pope Gregory IX's famous bull, the so-called magna carta of the University of Paris, Parens Scientiarum' (Traver 1997: 16). As the consequence of such feuds between academia, the city authorities and the monarchy, the Paris university model reached Cambridge and subsequently the United States (with the creation of colleges such as Harvard and others) and beyond. Hence, when their academic freedom was constrained, academics responded by moving elsewhere and setting up a new university in which they could enjoy academic freedom. Thus the ability to enjoy academic freedom became the *raison d'être* of the major mediaeval universities in Europe, so that academic freedom became a cornerstone of the modern research university: as Menand (1996: 4, 6) points out 'academic freedom is not simply . . . a philosophical luxury, . . . it is the key legitimating concept of the entire enterprise'. Consequently, academic freedom has been protected in the constitutions and legislative frameworks of many countries, and was recognized in the 1997 UNESCO World Declaration on Higher Education, which declaimed that 'higher education institutions should: ensure . . . due respect for autonomy and academic freedom, as being normal and inherent in their functioning' (UNESCO 1997: 12f.).

What is academic freedom?

Despite the longevity of university institutions and the universality of their structures, practices and personnel, conceptualizing academic freedom is surprisingly problematic. As has been seen, the theoretical and functional foundations of academic freedom find their roots in the first universities' struggles for autonomy in mediaeval Europe. However, as Goldstein points out, 'the modern development of the doctrine of academic freedom is largely derived from the nineteenth century German concepts of Lehrfreiheit and Lernfreiheit' (Goldstein 1976: 1293) which are associated with the reforms instituted at the University of Berlin by Wilhelm von Humboldt, whose concepts subsequently provided the template for the modern university across Europe and beyond. As Metzger accurately relates, *Lehrfreiheit*

> meant that the university professor was free to examine bodies of evidence and to report his findings in lecture or published form – that he enjoyed freedom of teaching and freedom of inquiry. This freedom was the distinctive prerogative of the academic profession, and the essential condition of all universities. (Metzger 1987: 1269)

Additionally, *Lehrfreiheit* referred to 'the statutory right of full and associate professors to decide on the content of their lectures and to publish the findings of their research without seeking prior ministerial or ecclesiastical approval or fearing state or church reproof' (Metzger 1987: 1269).

The concept of *Lernfreiheit* referred to 'learning freedom' under which, as Helmholtz relates, 'students had perfect freedom to migrate from one university to another; and in each university they had free choice among teachers of the same subject' (Helmholtz 1877: 333). However, this freedom was tempered by the unity of teaching and research (*Einheit von Lehre und Forschung*), which was a central aspect of the Humboldtian model. Consequently although students had considerable freedom to move from one class to another, deciding for themselves which courses to study, they were expected to engage actively with the resident scholars in the learning process. Thus 'working in the vineyard of knowledge side by side with his master, the student learnt the methods of his discipline and undertook his own investigations' (Hofstadter and Metzger 1955: 373).

The final aspect of academic freedom was self-governance and institutional autonomy which was constituted as 'the university's right, under the direction of its senior professors organized into separate faculties and a common senate to control its internal affairs' (Metzger 1987: 1270f.). This right was considered essential to protect the academic freedoms of teaching and research, as without such protection,

> the university . . . would be dangerously vulnerable to government or religious censorship. Without broad institutional powers, the academic Gelehrten [staff] would be at the mercy of the state or church. . . . [hence] institutional autonomy was indispensable to academic freedom. (Metzger 1987: 1270f.)

The variations in the processes of university governance and autonomy that occur both within and between universities and nation states are such that any definition of academic freedom that encompasses them has limitations. However, concentrating on the core elements of teaching and research enables the derivation of a generic statement which makes the essential elements of the concept readily explicable and accessible. Knowledge is created by challenging, rather than accepting, orthodox ideas and beliefs, which means that, because of the nature of their work, academics are more naturally led in to conflict with governments and other seats of authority. Academics are responsible for many important scientific discoveries (in biology, chemistry, medicine etc.), and without their work, knowledge would not have advanced; many of the benefits which people enjoy today would not be possible. To allow academics to challenge existing knowledge and create new ideas, they are granted the freedom to undertake research and discuss new ideas and problems of their discipline, and express their conclusions, through both publications and in the teaching of students, without interference from political or ecclesiastical authority, or from the administrative officials of their institution, unless their methods are found by qualified bodies within their own discipline to be clearly incompetent or contrary to professional ethics. Hence academic freedom can be defined as:

> the absence of, or protection from, such restraints or pressures – chiefly in the form of sanctions threatened by state or church authorities or by the authorities, faculties, or students of colleges and universities, but occasionally also by other power groups in society – as are designed to create in the minds of academic scholars (teachers, research workers, and students in colleges and universities) fears and anxieties that may inhibit them from freely studying and investigating whatever they are interested in, and from freely discussing, teaching, or publishing whatever opinions they have reached. (Machlup 1955: 753)

This acknowledgement of the need for, and right of, academic freedom within universities, so long accepted, has come into question in recent decades. The central role of universities in sustaining the growth of the knowledge economy, through their research and provision of high level scientific training and qualifications, has attracted the attention of governments. Seeking to increase the growth in knowledge as a lever to greater national prosperity, governments have sought, via legislation and legerdemain, to determine the research priorities and teaching curricula of universities in conformance with national economic and educational policies. Changes to the law in the United

Kingdom and, more recently, in France and Denmark for example, have led to accusations that national governments are eroding academic freedom. In Denmark in May 2008 the *Magisterforening*, the Danish university teachers' and researchers' professional association, submitted a formal complaint to UNESCO over the Danish government's failure to meet the standards for academic freedom set out in UNESCO's 'Recommendation concerning the status of higher education teaching personnel' (1997), to which the Danish government had been a signatory. Additionally, the large increase in university student numbers, allied to the growing participation by private companies in university research projects and the accompanying belief that universities exhibit business inefficiencies, has led to calls for greater accountability for universities' expenditure of public money. This has been achieved via increased mangerialism within universities and more control of their activities, with a consequent dilution in academic freedom. This shift has been endorsed by the findings of national committees of inquiry, such as the Attali Report in France (Attali 1998), the Bricall Report in Spain (Bricall 2000) and the Dearing Report (NCIHE 1997) in the United Kingdom, which all recommended a shift in governance in higher education towards less collegial and more corporate management structures. In addition to these external factors, recent years have also seen strong criticisms voiced by scholars whose writings have cast doubt on the intellectual neutrality of the process of knowledge creation within the academy itself. Hence both internal and external forces have challenged the need for the continuation of academic freedom, the concept of which has been central to the idea of the university since mediaeval times. These developments lead one to pose the question: Is academic freedom within the contemporary university an essential liberty or an extravagant luxury?

Is academic freedom an essential liberty?

The need for academic freedom has been debated ever since universities were founded in the Middle Ages; attacks have come from many quarters and, most recently, from within the academy itself. However, in addition to being important to academics and the universities in which they work, it should be recognized that academic freedom also has a broader remit. Academic freedom is indicative of democratic values within the wider community and at societal level, as many scholars have noted. Rochford, for example, argues that:

> academic freedom is not for the benefit of the academic, or even of the institution. It is for the benefit of society at large, and society's failure to provide the environment in which this freedom can flourish will result in the loss of a valuable asset. (Rochford 2003: 259)

A similar argument is advanced by Bergan, who declares academic freedom to be 'the heart of democratic society ... a democratic society is hardly conceivable without ... academic freedom' (Bergan 2003: 49). Likewise Turner argues that:

> academic freedom stands as one of the freedoms which a free society should value, cherish and maintain. A society which erodes or abolishes it is destroying a part of its civilized values, and may go on to destroy the others. It has been wisely said that the first target of those who wish to set up dictatorships is freedom of speech, the freedom of academics included. (Turner 1988: 111)

Pritchard agrees that 'academic freedom is but a facet of freedom in the larger society and malaise in academe is related to, and symptomatic of, that in the body politic as a whole' and relates that 'academic freedoms are implicit rather than explicit in the United Kingdom ... The erosion of these freedoms in academe is merely a reflection of a constitutional crisis in the larger society' (Pritchard 1998: 123).

As a result, Allen (1988: 112) suggests that 'one of the services which universities can render is to provide serious and direct criticism of the society of which they are a part'. Moreover, as Burgess points out, this role is significant even in democratic states, for

> democratic governments can err. Popular demand may be foolish. Both can be arbitrary, unjust and capricious. A democratic society is a plural society, one in which criticism is welcome and alternatives possible. . . . Many of the greatest advances have been made against political oppression, popular indifference or worse. (Burgess 1979: 145)

Consequently, as Hernes contends,

> Professors have not just served as experts and attendants for the powerful which fed them. They have represented counter-expertise. Hence politicians and the powers that be have not always seen professors as easy to handle – or believed that their knowledge produces wisdom. (Hernes 1993: 270)

Sjoberg (1998) extends this argument by suggesting that academic freedom is also important in enabling university staff to criticize and hold private corporations to account for their actions. Hence academic freedom enables academics to provide expert criticism of both governments and the corporate sector, thereby ensuring that they are fully accountable for their actions, and strengthening democracy. In this sense, as Machlup (1955: 753) observed, 'academic freedom is a right of the people, not a privilege of a few.'

The academic freedom to determine what research to undertake, to decide which methods to adopt and to disseminate their research findings freely is considered essential to the growth of knowledge within society, and thereby human betterment. As Post (2006: 74) opines 'Freedom of research and publication is the core of academic freedom. It is the freedom that follows most directly from the social function of the university.' Academics are experts in their respective subjects, hence they (rather than other less expert groups like politicians or civil servants) are best able to determine where research is likely to yield new knowledge, and what methodological approaches are likely to be the most productive in creating new knowledge. Such arguments are premised on the belief that basic research has an intrinsic cultural value, and hence it is necessary for a civilized society to fund the pursuit of knowledge for its own sake. Hence academics pursue research to extend the boundaries of knowledge, in pursuit of a general public good; they are not primarily concerned with the practical applications of research, either in considering new avenues of research or assessing its outcomes.

In this respect research in universities is different from that undertaken in (say) the laboratories of 'for-profit' commercial companies. The academic community perceives its primary research role in terms of:

- pursuing collaborative basic experimental or theoretical research in order to acquire new knowledge of the underlying foundation of phenomena and observable facts, without any specific application or use in view;
- supporting a free exchange of ideas and information that result from research;
- guaranteeing academic freedom to enable objective enquiry;
- upholding the probity of research.

By contrast, industrial and commercial companies:

- engage in directed, applied research;
- endeavour to maintain the secrecy of industrial ideas and processes through patents and copyrights;
- attempt to defend a competitive market position through patented products.

Research in universities is often both long term and speculative, but has the potential to have wide-ranging impacts on people across the globe. For example, the discovery of the structure of DNA by Crick and Watson in 1953 created new disciplines like biotechnology, which have a wide range of applications in areas such as agriculture (genetically modified crops), medicine (genetically targeted drugs) and forensics (DNA profiling). Similarly the World Wide Web, invented by Sir Tim Berners-Lee in 1989 to disseminate the experimental results of the CERD Laboratory, has since had a revolutionary impact on many aspects of people's lives including education, publishing, entertainment and communication. Businesses are typically concerned with shorter timescales for research and development, and there is a risk that under commercial influence fundamental and long term research in universities would not be undertaken. Hence, for example, it took the philosopher Bertrand Russell and his colleague Alfred North Whitehead two years to research the *Principia Mathematica* (Whitehead and Russell 1973), but the development of the digital computer would have been impossible without it. Reviewing examples such as these, it is difficult to disagree with Horwitz's view that 'academic freedom is prized primarily because its contribution to truth-seeking will yield discoveries or insights that ultimately will benefit society at large' (Horwitz 2005: 484).

Academic freedom is necessary for teaching as well as research: academic staff, being best informed about their particular discipline, are best able to determine what to teach and how it should be taught. In exercising this freedom staff must undertake teaching to the highest possible professional standards and ensure that their teaching accurately reflects current developments and debates in their subjects in a fair and balanced fashion. Determining how this should be undertaken is problematic, which led the Supreme Court in the United States to declaim that:

> the classroom is peculiarly the 'marketplace of ideas'. The Nation's future depends upon leaders trained through wide exposure to that robust exchange of ideas which discovers truth 'out of a multitude of tongues, [rather] than through any kind of authoritative selection'. (Keyishian v. Board of Regents 1967: 603)

Implicit in the notion of the classroom as a 'marketplace of ideas' is the Humboldtian ideal of the unity of teaching and research, and the collaborative pursuit of these by staff and students.

Is academic freedom an extravagant luxury?

Arguments for academic freedom have been voiced ever since universities were established. However, the research role of universities is comparatively recent and started within German universities following Humboldt's reforms. In the United Kingdom by contrast Newman contended as late as 1853 that

> to discover and to teach are distinct functions; they are also distinct gifts, and are not commonly found united in the same person. He, too, who spends his day in dispensing his existing knowledge to all comers is unlikely to have either leisure or energy to acquire new. (Newman 1853: 10)

Similarly, before the Second World War universities in the United States played a relatively minor role in the nation's scientific enterprise. However Roosevelt believed that the critical role of university scientists in winning the war could be extended to provide peacetime benefits. Hence in 1945 Vannevar Bush published the influential report *Science: The Endless Frontier* (Bush 1945), which signalled a major expansion in the role of research universities in the United States, and the consequent need for academic freedom. Bush argued that it would be self-defeating to try to constrain the creativity of basic research, and that scientific research was most productive if it was not under direct governmental control.

Assessing such claims for academic freedom for research realistically, Yudof (1987: 842) points out that studies in the United States found that:

> one-third of all professors admit to spending no time at all on research, while more than half spend less than five hours a week on it. . . . 60% of a sample of 5000 professors had never published or even edited a book in their subject areas.

Similarly, a Carnegie Foundation study found that 60 per cent of the professoriate in the United States reported their interests as lying with teaching rather than research, 56 per cent had never published or edited a book, 59 per cent had published in total no more than five journal articles, while 26 per cent had published nothing at all (Boyer 1990: Appendix A). Assessing such data, in combination with case studies by Trow and Fulton (1974) and others, leads Oakley (1997: 51) to conclude that 'the faculty member . . . places much higher priority on teaching and a lower priority on research than is usually alleged and nearly always assumed to be the case'. Similarly in the United Kingdom, the NCIHE found such a low level of research activity in some universities that it recommended amending the national Research Assessment Exercise to encourage some institutions to forgo submitting their research for assessment and instead seek non-competitive funding to support only research and scholarship which underpinned teaching (NCIHE 1997). Additionally, on the basis of a cross-European analysis, Enders and de Weert (2004: 20) relate that the Humboldtian premise that teaching and research are combined has come under pressure and in 'some universities . . . work patterns of academic staff . . . have been disentangled, such as the designation of teaching-only and research-only staff', with the former no longer requiring academic freedom in respect to their research activities. Such findings lead Shils to argue that:

> it is frequently said that originality of discovery and analysis is inhibited or suppressed where there is no right of academic freedom, . . . I think that this is not straight forward. Most cases of infringement of academic freedom have nothing to do with original thought or discovery. Most academics are not capable of original thought or discovery. (Shils 1995: 7)

With respect to teaching, Post (2006: 79) notes that 'academic freedom in the classroom is an exceedingly complex and ill-defined topic' – which makes it more difficult to justify. Within the Humboldtian model, the unity of teaching and research requires that academic freedom is necessary to allow the professor to determine how to teach and what is to be taught. However, the belief that academic staff know the best way to teach their subject, and therefore need academic freedom for this function, is increasingly coming into question. Laurillard (2002: 3) for example notes that 'There is no professional training requirement for university academics in terms of their teaching competence,' so expecting an academic who is an expert in his own field to be aware of new research in teaching and learning is as unrealistic as assuming that he will be conversant with recent research into any other specialism. Consequently, as Collis (1999: 39) notes, 'many may not be aware that there is an extensive base of theory and research related to the science of teaching and learning in higher education.' Moreover, university lecturers view themselves as professionals with responsibility for determining their own professional development needs, so even where they recognize that they may need to alter their mode of teaching they may be loath to do so – as Elton (1994: 9) wryly observes: 'it is one of the paradoxes of academia that while universities provide training and development for every other profession, there is a reluctance for academics to recognize the need for it for themselves.' More important than an aversion to admitting the requirement for teacher training is the continuing emphasis on research, rather than teaching, for career progression. MacFarlane (WPCSUP 1992: 2) points to the crux of the matter: 'The greatest challenge is to persuade a majority of those involved in higher education to see teaching as their prime activity, posing intellectual challenges and offering rewards comparable to those of standard research.' Until such time as teaching is deemed to be as important as research in determining career progression, academics are unlikely to alter their modes of teaching from traditional so-called chalk and talk methods. Consequently, continuing to allow academics freedom to determine how they teach may lead to inadequate learning by students.

Conclusion

The relatively low level of research by academics and their lack of teacher training represent cogent arguments in favour of restricting academic freedom. However, the major criticism of academic freedom in the last decade has come from within the academy and is centred on the very nature of both knowledge itself and academic inquiry. The modernist notion of academic inquiry, dating back to the Enlightenment, assumes that facts exist and that it is the academic's job to further the boundaries of knowledge by uncovering these facts through research. Implicit in this scheme are the ideas that the university is a 'marketplace of ideas' and that research is objective and independent, with the production of knowledge untainted by the ideology or personal beliefs of the researcher. However, based on the work of Foucault and other post-modernists, Tierney and others have argued that the 'production of knowledge is socially constructed . . . institutions, individuals and the constantly shifting social forces of society combine to determine what accounts for knowledge'. (Tierney 1993: 148). More critically, philosophers like Rorty (1996: 24) have argued that 'there is nothing to objectivity except inter-subjectivity' thus 'it is pointless to ask whether reality is independent of our ways of talking about it' which leads him to assert 'there are lots of different philosophical beliefs about the nature of truth and rationality that can be invoked to defend the traditions of "academic freedom", and that in the short run at least, it does not greatly matter which ones we pick' (Rorty 1996: 24). This argument negates the rationale for academic freedom, given that, as Menand points out:

> A professor who believes that 'truth' is simply a name for what a particular group finds it advantageous to regard as given or universal . . . can hardly have much use for a concept grounded on the premise that intellectual inquiry is a neutral and disinterested activity. (Menand 1996: 12)

Furthermore, Searle argues,

> the biggest single consequence of the rejection of the Western Rationalist Tradition is that it makes possible an abandonment of traditional standards of objectivity, truth and rationality, and opens the way for an educational agenda one of whose primary purposes is to achieve social and political transformation [with the result that] in the case of Women's Studies, and several other such new disciplines . . . The new departments often thought of their purpose, at least in part, as advancing certain moral and political causes. (Searle 1993: 72f.)

In this sense post-modernism undermines both academic freedom and the university itself – as Haskell (1996: 70) pointedly asks, if 'there is no respectable sense in which we are entitled to say that there is a "nature of things" for inquirers to "get right", then one cannot help wondering what the community of inquiry is for'.

In rebutting such fundamental attacks on academic freedom such as these, some have questioned the academic credibility of the post-modernists. Scull (2007: 3), for example, assessing the *History of Madness* (Foucault 2005) found Foucault's 'elaborate intellectual constructions are built on the shakiest of empirical foundations'. A major problem in responding to such post-modernist attacks, Searle finds, is that it is

> very difficult to find any clear, rigorous and explicit arguments against the core elements of the Western Rationalist Tradition. . . . Sometimes we are said to be in a postmodern era, . . . but this alleged change is often treated as if it were like a change in the weather, something that just happened without need or argument or proof. (Searle 1993: 77)

However, attacking the philosophical foundations of post-modernism head on, Dworkin (1996: 139) concludes his own impressive assault by stating:

> When we are told that whatever convictions we do struggle to reach cannot in any case be true or false, or objective, or part of what we know, or that they are

just moves in a game of language, . . . or just experimental projects we should try
for size or just invitations to thoughts that we might find diverting or amusing or
less boring than the ways we used to think, we must reply that these denigrating
suggestions are all false, just bad philosophy.

More pragmatically, Rabban contends that 'protecting the academic freedom of professors . . . fosters knowledge about the world that benefits society.
Despite their skepticism about achieving objective and permanent truths, a
significant proportion of post-modern thinkers agree' (Rabban 1998: 1398),
thus indicating that challenges to the basis of knowledge cannot themselves
flourish without freedom of debate and discourse.

Like other basic rights, such as democracy, academic freedom has demon-
strable deficiencies, although these are outweighed by its proven benefits.
Allowing academic freedom to be diminished threatens the proper functioning of universities and the rightful activities of their staff. Furthermore, if
academic freedom is no longer considered an essential liberty, other broader
freedoms enjoyed by society may also come to be considered as extravagant
luxuries. Hence as Shiell points out, 'although academic freedom for teachers
and professors is a set of rights (and responsibilities) assigned to individuals,
the rights (and responsibilities) are justified not through their value to that
individual but through their value to society' (Shiell 2006: 40).

3 Learning Landscapes: Designing a Classroom of the Future

Mike Neary and Angela Thody

Introduction

In the recent period universities have become increasingly aware of the importance of their built environment for making a statement about their institutional mission. This appreciation of the importance of the quality of the university estate has coincided with developments in information technology which have given campus designers another level of dimensionality by which to create places for teaching, learning and research. This adds layers of sophistication and complexity to spaces that provide for traditional and newly emerging pedagogies.

This chapter explores these new developments in higher education through the idea of learning landscapes, a concept that has emerged as a way of thinking holistically about the refurbishment and rebuilding of universities. While, as the chapter makes clear, there is no real agreement or simple definition as to the precise meaning of the learning landscape, the use of a metaphor of this kind allows for a level of conceptualization about the construction of universities which can make a significant contribution to the debate about the future of higher education.

And yet the debate about the future of the university is not simply concerned with the shape of the built environment, but includes questions about the nature and idea of the university itself. In order to engage with these issues it is important for universities to ensure that the buildings they create are compatible with the academic and intellectual sensibilities on which the idea of the university is founded.

This is no small undertaking, and yet the grandeur of this ambition need not be articulated in iconic buildings or campus master plans, but can be expressed in modest ways on the university estate. This chapter provides an example of a classroom designed as an intelligent and intellectual space for teaching and learning, and, as such, a site through which to challenge conventional wisdom about curriculum design, the nature of the relationship between academic and student, and, through the ways in which it poses these questions, the future of higher education itself.

Space and spatiality

The teaching and learning environment is being redesigned at all levels of the educational system in the United Kingdom, with the issue of space and spatiality now central to any discussions about the nature of teaching and learning (Edwards and Usher 2003; Hutchinson 2004). At school level this is being taken forward by the *Building Schools for the Future* initiative, sponsored by the national government; at the level of higher education, this work is being driven by capital funding from the Higher Education Funding Councils for England and Wales and the Scottish Funding Council, all of whom are supporting redevelopment across the sector (SFC 2006; JISC 2003–2007), as well as providing monies for specific building programmes, including the Centres for Excellence for Teaching and Learning (**www.hefce. ac.uk/learning/tinits/cetl/**).

A key issue in this capital building programme is the relationship between architectural design and pedagogy. While it is logical to suppose that teaching and learning should drive design (Jamieson 2003), in practice architectural design and pedagogy appear disconnected (Barnett and Temple 2006), with architectural imperatives coming before any *raisons d'être* for teaching and learning (Edwards 2000). Conversely, the literature on higher education pedagogy tends to ignore architectural issues (Temple 2007).

Not only is there a disconnect between design and pedagogy, but the matter of space itself is undertheorized. Despite the fact that no space is 'intellectually neutral' (Temple 2007: 37), the literature on the redesign of teaching and learning spaces fails to deal with the ways in which space has been conceptualized by intellectuals within universities:

> The architectural theorising on space seems mainly to consist of post-hoc attempts to explain what it is that architects are doing when they design spaces: it is not clear that such theorising actually guides architects in their work. (Temple 2007: 17)

The lack of engagement in the conceptualization of university spaces is ironic, as interest and enquiry into space and spatiality is a mainstream activity within universities. Writing on aspects of space can be found throughout the social sciences, the humanities, the arts and in the natural sciences, in particular physics, where thinking about space and its relationship to time has fundamentally transformed the spatial consciousness of humanity (Miller 2001).

Temple (2007) insists that it must be possible to conceive of a body of theoretical work on space that can be used to inform the debates about the design of learning spaces for the twenty-first century. He cites the work of spatial theorists – including Lefebvre and his 'science of space', as well as some critical responses to this work by Foucault and Derrida – as exemplars of thinkers who might inform such a discussion; but, having encouraged a deeper understanding of the spatiality of teaching environments, Temple does not develop this line of enquiry.

Hubbard et al. (2007) provide a useful framework on which to base a theoretical understanding of space. The traditional approaches to writing about space have been based within a Newtonian framework of absolute space: an empty void, without a history or a future, in which people and things move and react, driven by a force that is measurable and predictable, but cannot be explained by reference to the logic of the space itself. This thinking about space was transformed by the Einsteinian revolution where the relationship between space and time was recast with the theory of relativity. The significance of this theory is that space and time can no longer be regarded as absolute and fixed; but, rather, space and time have an origin and a dynamic that is derived out of the relationship between the matter and energy by which the space is constituted. What this means is that space and time are amenable to human ingenuity, and can be affected by human activity. Space and time do not simply exist, but can be made and remade.

It was out of these new conceptualizations of space that the work of Lefebvre (1991) emerged. His work was the 'big bang' moment in the formation of a history of social space. For Lefebvre, social space is the product of whatever social relations of production are dominant at the moment in which the space is made. Modern space is, therefore, capitalist space, constructed according to the logic of capitalist accumulation, which includes the need to control and dominate labour power.

According to Lefebvre, if space could be made, it could also be remade. He argued that space was neither fixed nor absolute, but was a site on which to explore the endless potential of human capability. But if Lefebvre provided a liberatory understanding of space, his theory was disabled by its failure to come to terms with the fact that space is neither open nor flexible and that spatial ideas must be materialized in real space and real time (Harvey 2000).

While Lefebvre provided a framework for an historical and structural conceptualization of how space is made, subsequent theories of space have sought to emphasize the more subjective processes by which space is conceived. These processes include human memory, imagination and the ways in which meaning is attributed to particular spaces. In these approaches to the making of space, the concept of space is often replaced or re-presented by the concept of place (Massey 2007).

Associated with these more personal accounts of space formation are theorizations which privilege the notion of embodiment: the ways in which people exist in and through space. Particular emphasis is made within these theories of embodiment to the ways in which spaces and places are gendered (Rose 1993) and racialized (hooks 1984, 1990). These theories of embodiment are not only concerned with cognitive functions but also the ways in which non-cognitive capacities interpret space and place, including the full range of sensory perceptions and our instinctive sense of being in the world, encompassing our 'animality' and 'undeadness' (Thrift 2008). These more private and personal accounts of space look for ways to find significance for our relationships with the mundane and familiar: 'the thing world' (Thrift 2008). This form of thinking about the spatial world, which is described as non-representational theories of space (Thrift 2008), has shifted the emphasis of social theory away from representation and interpretation, to focus on 'performative embodied knowledges' as they occur in an ever changing structure of time and place (Hubbard et al. 2007); and, in so doing, non-representational theory provides another sort of 'thinking space' to think about the concept of space.

Learning landscapes: terminological exactitude or confusion?

Recently the metaphor of the learning landscape has emerged to provide a content for this 'thinking space', and a framework for conceptualizing the spaces of teaching and learning. The strength of this metaphor is that it encourages a holistic approach to a set of very complex processes.

The concept of learning landscapes has been used by educational theorists to contextualize processes of change in education, and has now been extended to deal with the transformation of university environments

(Noyes 2002; Serafin 2006). The concept has been taken over by designers of academic spaces to rethink the learning experiences that occur in virtual as well as physical space. In the context of learning landscapes learning can happen in a wide variety of places, supported by a matrix of information systems, wireless access and mobile devices, which provide a mesh of discovery between students, faculty staff and the wider community (DEGW 2007).

Studies from the world of business define learning landscapes as 'mechanisms that enable project-to-project learning to take place' (Brady et al. 2002: 11–12). These mechanisms involve mapping exercises across educational sites (Starik et al. 2002) as a way of acquiring data about the use of learning environments. Such mapping projects are ongoing at the Universities of Cambridge and Oxford Brookes, and across various parts of the higher education sector (ETL 2002–2005; Francis and Raftery 2005; Lytras et al. 2005). These maps include personal learning landscapes (Russell et al. 1998; Tosh and Werdmuller 2004), group and social learning environments (Francis and Raftery 2005; JISC 2003–2007), the whole university campus (DEGW 2006; Chiddick 2007) and beyond, envisioning twenty-first century universities as new towns, established to house increasingly diverse, mass student populations in central hubs electronically linked for any-real-time learning to suburban and rural centres.

Learning landscapes are not only about the future, but are also about symbolic linkages to the past, since universities have been societal conservators as well as leading futurologists (Kerr 1999; Starik et al. 2002). Just as the Romantic movement added cultural aestheticism to university goals with an interest in the significance of the beauty of buildings for the learning process (Hendley 2002), the learning landscapes agenda intends to create inspirational environments through the 'wow factor' of good architecture (Chiddick 2006).

The concept of learning landscapes is often 'partisan and ideologically charged' (Hutchinson 2004: 14). With the change from an elite to a mass educational system in the United Kingdom, different types of learning interactions are being created through every possible means of contact with staff, peers and with communities and businesses connected to the university (Brennan and Jary 2005). This approach to the idea of learning landscapes stresses that these different kinds of connections need robust models through which to express the pedagogies on which they are based. While the tradition of university architecture has been to focus on the mainstream power bases that house academic staff and administrators, the concept of learning landscapes reminds us that a more holistic approach, taking into account issues of equality and diversity, including all university staff and governors, is needed to fit with the more expansive approaches to the learning landscapes agenda (Bourgeois and Frenay 2001).

Among the many debates about the desirability of these developments (Smith 1999: 163–6), there seems to be a general agreement that learning is most effective when it is self-initiated and interconnected. This is recognized in the realization that students add informality to a university's structured learning spaces, colonizing corridors and cafés (Brennan and Osborne 2005), neatly categorized as 'the bits in-between' (DEGW 2006; Arthur and Lindsay 2006). This approach to learning landscapes suggests that a new politics of space is needed to encourage student activity (Terenzini 2005), that is both 'flexible and distributed' (Francis and Raftery 2005). This new politics of space could lead to the design of more 'proactive and broader learning land-scapes' (Dealty 2002), to produce 'constructive alignment' between course aims and their environments (ETL 2000/2001), where students are enabled to be fully engaged in the academic world (Barnett 2005b: 795).

These learning theories and practices are much enhanced by the new tech-nologies which are considered integral to the design of learning landscapes in universities, businesses and schools (JISC 2003–2007; Aldrich 2006; DEGW 2006). There is however a recognition that the virtual world of detached learn-ing experiences (Serafin 2006), needs to be supplemented with traditional learning modes (Chiddick 2006) and human interactions (Smith 1999) so as to decrease learning isolation (Sarles 2001; Chiddick 2006). So long as these caveats are recognized, the ubiquitized, immersive forms of e-learning can be installed around the whole university learning landscape and connect it to the external world (DEGW 2006).

Some reactions to these new landscapes are positive (Barnett 2005b). Others record negative responses (Gilbert 2000; Cutright 2001; Scruton 2001; Maskell and Robinson 2002). What is important is that the concept provides an opportunity to reflect on the values and objectives that are fundamental to a university education (Sarles 2001).

The strength of the learning landscape metaphor is that it captures the 'architecture of complexity' (Temple 2007: 69) that underpins the redesign of teaching and learning in higher education in the United Kingdom. In order for this redesign to realize its full potential, however, it needs to connect with the intellectual project, 'the thinking space', within which issues about space and spatiality are being rethought.

This is not a classroom: a machine for teaching

Rethinking the learning landscape includes both whole campuses and individual learning spaces within them. Several universities have developed small-scale projects which attempt to connect the design of a learning space with the ways in which we think about the places in which academics teach. One such example is the Reinvention Centre at Warwick University. Here, a teaching space was opened in 2007 which was designed in an open dialogue with the theories and conceptualizations of space and place.

The Reinvention Centre is a Centre for Excellence for Teaching and Learning, based in the Sociology department at Warwick and working in collaboration with the School of the Built Environment at Oxford Brookes University. The purpose of the Centre is to support and promote the development of research-based learning in the undergraduate curricula.

The problem for the Centre was how to design a space that allowed for closer collaboration between student and teacher. Key to the Reinvention Centre's commitment to research-based learning is a critical pedagogy which challenges the idea of students as passive consumers of education and emphasizes the importance of their being active producers of real knowledge and an integral part of the research culture of departments and universities (Freire 1970; Rancière 1991). In this model, hierarchical relationships between student and teacher are transformed to produce more fluid and elaborate collaborations between producers of scholarly work. Addressing these theoretical issues in practical ways calls for a critical rethinking and reinvention of the spaces in which students learn: the Reinvention Centre's teaching space has been designed in order to offer a creative response to these demands (Lambert 2008).

The teaching space is a rectangular block: 120 square metres of light and colour, stripped of all decoration – white walls, blue rubber floor, primary colour cubed seats, round yellow bean bags and long monochrome grey and black benches. There are no tables and chairs, nor is there any obtrusive technology, only Ethernet connection points, electric sockets around the walls and a Wi-Fi capability. There are no screens or projectors to create focal points where the teacher might stand to deliver a lecture. The space is lit by a sophisticated lighting system, including spotlights set in the floor that shine up through the rafters into a slanted roof.

The design principles that inform the space are rooted in intellectual conceptualizations of space and spatiality, including the leitmotifs of non-representational theory. By borrowing ideas from non-representational theory it is possible to see the teaching space as a 'site' that is 'an active and always incomplete incarnation of events, an actualization of times and spaces that uses the fluctuating conditions to assemble itself' (Kwon 2004, in Thrift 2008: 12). The teaching space brings some of the key preoccupations of non-representational theory to life. Stripped of its tables and chairs the room is not for sitting in for long periods, but has been designed as 'a celebration of movement . . . the joy of living' (Thrift 2008: 5). The teaching space captures the joy of learning, and 'a certain attitude to life as potential' (Thrift 2008: 5), and a 'jump towards another world' (Thrift 2008: 15). This attitude to life and learning is not based merely within the cognitive aspects of teaching, but includes a recognition of the importance of different states of knowing and not-knowing, or precognition, that is, body language, where the emphasis is on a recognition of the ambient self (Thrift 2008: 12). This is a serious space, but the colours and shapes of the furniture emphasize a playful sensibility, recognizing that there are ways to learn ethics, values and responsibility through activities that are serious, yet enjoyable and fun (Thrift 2008: 12). And, like non-representational theory, the classroom is experimental, pulling 'the energy of the performing arts into the social sciences' (Thrift 2008: 12). The room reflects this type of aspiration with leaning rails, like a dance studio. The room melds the energy of the performing arts with not only the energy of fine art, but with its critical sensibility.

This artistic sensibility is seen through the ways in which art is used to inform the teaching space. The artistic influences on the teaching space are Purism and Neoplasticism, Utopian art movements that emerged in the 1920s as a protest against the chaotic carnage of the First World War. Purism, or Cubism without the decoration, is noted for its 'geometric forms and large areas of colour' as well as its 'cool and detached paint surfaces' (en.wikipedia. org/wiki/Purism). Purism's critique of the mass killing of the First World War lay in its emphasis on 'careful, compositional, chromatic order' (www. humanitiesweb.org/human.php?s/g&p=a&a=i&ID=508) based on the logic of modern machines. The main exponent of Purism was Le Corbusier; the teaching space contains a replica of his seminal chaise longue, designed in 1928 with other Purist artists and known as the 'relaxing machine' (en.wikipedia.org/wiki/Le_Corbusier).

Neoplasticism is a more extreme form of Purism, stripped down to the barest elements of design with no recognizable figurative content. The main proponent of Neoplasticism was Piet Mondrian. High up on one of the walls of the teaching space is a plexiglass and aluminium sculpture, by Liam Gillick: a neoplastic piece in the style of Mondrian. Gillick says of the materials he works with: 'Plexiglass and aluminium are the materials of renovation and refurbishment. They are the materials of McDonald's signs, and display cases in Prada, of aeroplanes and bullet-proof screens in banks, of really sexy nightclub floors and riot shields' (education.guardian.co.uk/higher/arts/story/0,,711242,00.html).

Not something you would normally find in a university classroom.

As for technology, the room has state of the art audio visual equipment, set on wheels and transportable around the space, providing multiple points of focus and disturbing the traditional one-dimensional lecture-style lines of sight. These multiple sight-lines undermine the concept of classrooms built around the traditional idea of perspective that creates not only a focal point, but establishes the teacher as the dominant presence within the room. Taking into account these powerful dynamics of space, the room is organized so that there are no obvious places for the teacher or the student: each space needs to be negotiated and claimed (Rose 1993). This lack of a dominating focal point reflects the cubist anti-perspectival sensibility, consolidating the Utopian tendency of the room which presents the future as something to be constructed rather than ready-made. There is no fear of the future in this space: no 'future-proofing' (Miller 2001).

If the space is informed by non-representational theory, it is, at the same time, engaged in a critical dialogue with the world of the non-representational. While the ideas that inform non-representational theory are heavily influenced by post-structuralism, the teaching space is fixated on the world of the real. In other words, the space is grounded in the historical materiality of a real world that can be known. This embeddedness in the real world is manifest by the significance given to the area that acts as a reality-check for the whole room: the floor. The floor provides a sense of gravitas and gravity for the entire space. The floor is a surface for working on as well as walking on. The floor is heated and rubberized, providing an all-around feeling of warmth and comfort. By making the floor more than something to be trampled on, the space recognizes the significance of the floor as a site of social interaction, and, with its emphasis on the symbolic importance of the floor, is a reminder of the ways in which floor space is used by other cultures, giving the room a racial and ethnic intelligence (hooks 1984, 1990).

Utopia?

While non-representational theory suggests an empathy with the modern world and an aspiration to move into the future, it gives no convincing framework as to how this advancement might be made. Spatial theories that are embedded in the historically material find this framework for moving into the future through a critical engagement with Lefebvre's 'science of space'. Lefebvre's problem was how to design a space that allows for the endless possibility of space and time without at the same time shutting down that sense of experiment through the construction of a permanent space. Harvey (2000) finds the solution in what he refers to as 'dialectic utopianism'. He argues that spaces which enable life to be felt differently are made by confronting the contradiction between closure and endless experimentation.

This idea of 'dialectial utopianism' is made real in the classroom by the work of Barnett (2007) who suggests a dialectic formula through which university spaces can be remade: he refers to this approach as 'critical utopianism' (Barnett 2007: 4). Barnett finds this dialectic in the *pedagogical* and *curricula spaces* of higher education. Pedagogical space is the room for alternative forms of teaching, while curricula spaces are those already made by the formal requirements of university programmes. For Barnett, pedagogical spaces are defined by 'freedom, a key concept deep within the idea of higher education', where 'students can become authentically themselves' (Barnett 2007: 141). But within such spaces come risks or a 'fear of freedom' (Barnett 2007: 139). For the teacher this is manifest in a disinclination to surrender control, a worry that not all of the syllabus will be covered, the undermining of the teacher's authority, or that the student may fail. The student may fear the open-endedness of the curricula, with too much responsibility and not enough structure, may be reticent about assuming a more dominant role or be driven by a more instrumental approach to their study (Barnett 2007: 140).

Evaluation

In the Reinvention Centre's teaching space this dialectic is made real by the design of the activities that take place between the pedagogical and curricula space.

In ongoing evaluations of the work that goes on in the teaching space some students who use the space say it is 'uncomfortable', but they also find the space challenging and interesting. They like the fact that 'it is not the usual boring teaching room', and, therefore 'allows for unstructured lessons'. They recognize that the space 'promotes active and interactive learning', as well as allowing for critical thinking: 'It makes you realise you can think outside the box' in a way that 'breaks boundaries'. The students enjoy the excitement and stimulation that the room adds to their learning experience, and the fact that it is part of a larger project outside their own student experience. As one student put it, the teaching space is 'the first step towards something big!' (http://www2.warwick.ac.uk/fac/soc/sociology/research/cetl/spaces/westwood/)

Students are positive about the alternative forms of pedagogy used in the space, in particular research-based learning:

> I really like it, I must admit that I was a bit edgy about it, I thought I don't know about this, but from the first time we went into the room I knew it was going to work. I do think it is a really good way of learning, rather than superficially glossing over lots of issues. I think the process has worked pretty well, the structure is quite loose, but I like that, I really like it. (Student 1, interview with author – March 2007)

> I think it's a really good idea, with freedom to develop ideas and to get involved. In normal lectures and seminars there is no real input from the student, it's more like school, where you are told what to do and what to write, but this is more like proper research, encouraging new ideas and not depended on secondary material. It makes everything more diverse and the module is very much student led, everyone has real input and can make lots of different suggestions in a more relaxed and productive environment. The world has changed and it is important that methods of teaching reflect that change. (Student 2, interview with author – March 2007)

Teachers appreciate the technical capacity of the space:

> The Reinvention Centre has finally allowed me to undertake the flexible, responsive and research-led teaching that I have always wanted to pursue. The room's non-hierarchical configuration permits a relaxed and continually varied atmosphere in which to explore ideas across a variety of media; so far we have used it for viewing and discussing film, video, still images and texts. I have found that its resources work particularly well in collaboration with Warwick's e-learning facilities (especially blogs and podcasts), so that the weekly seminar becomes an informed forum for debating independent research, rather than a one-way download of information from teacher to student. (Teacher 1, Neary et al. 2007)

They also enjoy its sense of creativity and its inventive ambition:

> What creative people need is open space – a space where everything is possible, and endlessly possible, the space for error and experiment. For a writer, teaching

and learning in The Reinvention Centre is like working on an open page. It holds potential as a creative open space, and offers room for error, experiment and astonishing achievement. (Teacher 2, Neary et al. 2007)

In the education press the space has been recognized as persuading students to move 'out of their comfort zone' (education.guardian.co.uk/egweekly/story/0,,2191536,00.html). It is acknowledged that the Reinvention Centre classroom is capable of giving 'a more lasting jolt to teaching on British campuses' as well as providing a teaching space within which 'the learning mould is smashed'. (education.independent.co.uk/higher/article2141953.ece) and (education.independent.co.uk/higher/article2141963.ece).

Conclusion

The issue of space and spatiality is now at the centre of how universities are thinking about designing their built environments. It is clear that in order for this process to be successful it needs to involve not only architects, planners and other service providers, but also the academic community and students. It is important that this level of engagement involves a relationship between the design and the academic ambition of the university. The concept of learning landscape is a useful instrument for dealing with these levels of engagement in ways that are both practical and theoretical, including the whole university community. But, as with all concepts and theories, in order for them to maintain their vitality and dynamism they need to be subject to the most rigorous and robust critiques, so that the landscape within which the learning takes place is constantly renewed and reinvigorated.

It is important that these critical discussions are not simply conducted as abstract debates, but that academics have a real opportunity to engage with the development of the material spaces within which they teach. In order for this to happen universities need to find ways to accommodate the voices of academics and students within their formal planning processes and protocols. New teaching and learning spaces can then be grounded in a process which is informed by architectural design principles, the most resilient protocols of estate management and the robust demands of academic scholarship.

Learning and Teaching for Sustainable Development in Higher Education: Examining Dissonance and Instructional Strategy

4

Terfot Ngwana

Introduction

In the past 20 years Education for Sustainable Development (ESD) has attracted a wide range of scholarly and political interest following the publication of the 1987 Brundtland report, which outlined the findings of the World Commission on Environment and Development. Indeed most definitions of both sustainability and sustainable development draw their inspiration from it (Kagawa 2007). Sustainable development is defined in the report as 'development that meets the needs of the present without compromising the ability of the future generations to meet their needs' (WCED 1987: 43). Sustainability, on the other hand, is described by Cortese (1999) as a condition whereby all present and future generations can afford good health, fulfil their basic needs, have a fair and equitable access to the world's resources, have a decent quality of life and preserve the biologically diverse ecosystem on which everyone depends. In this chapter sustainability will be defined as a goal, while sustainable development will be taken to mean a means of attaining such a goal (Buchan et al. 2007). This is in line with the conception that sustainability is evolving and that education has a transformational role in sustainable development (Kagawa 2007; Murray and Murray 2007; Roberts and Roberts 2007).

This chapter explores a specific learning and teaching model intended to influence the attitude of learners and teachers towards education for or about sustainable development. The international and national contexts of the development of sustainability and sustainable development are examined and used both as the premise for proposing the centrality of sustainable development in education, and as a relevant model of learning and teaching in higher education. It is also an attempt to provide a theoretical and practical reflection on the difficulties facing educators in translating sustainability into a popular culture for learners and teachers in higher education. The rationale is based on the fact that in the United Kingdom and in the wider international community emphasis is placed on the role of education, in particular higher education, in sustainable development: a potentially seismic shift in the learning landscape.

However, creating and supporting sustainable development requires individual and collective positive action. It is already known that socialization and formal or informal education forms the foundation for attitudes towards both sustainability and sustainable development. However such processes can also produce dissonance. Dissonance is taken to mean a cognitive process that grapples with contradictory ideas which interfere with fundamental beliefs (www.learningandteaching.info/learning/dissonance.htm). Concepts of dissonance range from a simple disagreement with the content of a new idea to the definition provided by psychologists, who refer to it as cognitive dissonance: discomfort felt at a discrepancy between what is already known or believed and new information or interpretations (Atherton 2005). Such ambiguity towards sustainable development has been highlighted in Clugston and Calder (1999), Beckerman (1994) and Claxton (1994).

The fact that practitioners – academics or policy advisers – are operating against a backdrop of potential or real dissonance has been observed by Roberts and Roberts (2007), where students in higher education demonstrate dissonance either by way of not being convinced, or by not adapting their actions to take account of their knowledge (Claxton 1994). This dissonance between theory and practice is exemplified in the following statements:

> Sustainability is really complicated, most people are never going to understand it, and most won't change their behaviour, business is just pretending.

> Now I realise the responsibility is everyone's but – I still want to be able to buy a fast car and have nice things. (Roberts and Roberts 2007: 18)

This embedded dissonance between theory and action was further demonstrated by Kagawa (2007), who found that while student attitudes towards sustainability were generally positive, there was a consistent pattern of mixed responses when it came to actions that affect personal lifestyle; relatively few would readily adapt their current lifestyle in favour of sustainable development, despite its being identified as a good thing. Similarly, the qualitative analysis by (Roberts and Roberts 2007) demonstrates that while 71.5 per cent of students think that sustainability is a positive idea, most may not be committed enough to implement corresponding life and professional changes. This highlights an embedded dissonance between theory and action, and hence the need for instructional or pedagogic approaches that address it. The implication is that the attitudes of students and teachers in higher education would be the best predictor of their change of behaviour with respect to the message of ESD. Based on this argument, the main objective of a corresponding instructional strategy would focus on refining attitude.

This chapter, therefore, explores the conceptual issues relating to dissonance before proposing an instructional approach that can be embedded in learning and teaching programmes in higher education. The conceptualization considered in this chapter is drawn from the literature that is generally supportive of sustainable development rather than the strand that questions the basis of it. The primary observation is that analysts who address attitudes towards sustainable development approach the task in two significantly different ways: either as an *issue* (assuming an underlying fundamental disagreement), or as a *problem* (a generally accepted enigmatic situation with an illusive solution). Both approaches are characterized by the use of scientific justifications to develop arguments. Cortese (1999), for instance, states that sustainability can only be accessible if there is a dramatic change in our current mindset and behaviour. Though the knowledge base may be convincing, this argument presupposes that there is an inbuilt opposition to it. Onwueme and Borsari (2007) on the other hand use the problem approach and propose that less antagonistic language should be used in addressing attitudes towards sustainability. This subtle differentiation poses specific challenges for the development of learning and teaching approaches in higher education, many of which have been recognized in a number of significant international reports.

International and national contexts of sustainable development and higher education

The last quarter of the twentieth century witnessed a steady rise in the level of international consensus on sustainable development in general and ESD in particular. In 1983, the UN General Assembly adopted Resolution 38/161 to appoint a commission to examine issues related to sustainability by the year 2000 and beyond. The resolution was in response to concerns expressed by social and natural scientists about the interrelationship between people, resources, environment and other aspects of development. Based on the knowledge provided in support of these concerns, the World Commission on Environment and Development, chaired by Gro Harlem Brundtland, was convened. The main terms of reference for the commission were to:

- define a shared perception and appropriate efforts to deal with environmental and developmental issues;
- recommend ways in which greater international co-operation could be used in achieving common goals on people, resources and environment;
- consider ways by which environmental issues can foster international co-operation irrespective of level of economic and social development.

The report, *Our Common Future*, (WCED 1987) has ever since constituted the fundamental international source of inspiration for the development sustainability and sustainable development projects at national and local levels.

Clugston and Calder (1999) describe how the WCED (1987) report was followed up by a series of conferences and declarations aimed at identifying specific directions for development. In terms of the relationship between ESD and higher education, two main international declarations are deemed most relevant for this chapter. One is the Talloires Declaration of 1990, signed by 22 university leaders to create a framework to encourage universities' role in developing a sustainable future. The other is the UN's Decade of Education for Sustainable Development (DESD) 2005–2014 (UNESCO 2005), which was adopted in 2002 as an international implementation scheme and was instrumental in establishing ESD as a key skill at all levels of education. These declarations highlight the key role of education in general, and universities in particular, in promoting sustainable development.

On a national scale, the range and emphasis of policy initiatives in the United Kingdom is an indication that there is an effort to endorse the international impetus on ESD (Kagawa 2007). In 1994 the government developed a strategy for sustainable development, with a detailed implementation proposal entitled *A Better Quality of Life*, published in 1999 by the Department for Food and Rural Affairs (DEFRA 1999). Following extensive consultation a revised version of the implementation strategy, *Securing the Future*, was published (DEFRA 2005). This coincided with the UN DESD; the recognition at national and international levels that education is a fundamental agency for attaining sustainability prompted DEFRA, which had so far led policy across government departments, to pass the responsibility for ESD to the (then) Department for Education and Skills. The specific framework for the implementation of the broad macro policy agenda is spelled out in key documents such as the Higher Education Environmental Performance Improvement project of 2001 (James and Hopkinson 2004), the Higher Education Partnership for Sustainable Development's guidelines for reporting for sustainability (HEPS 2003); and the Higher Education Academy's efforts to encourage all 24 subject centres to address ESD in their curriculum and to foster the further development of sustainability through the Education for Sustainable Development Project (www.heacademy.ac.uk/ourwork/learning/sustainability). It is worth noting that these policy development initiatives are just as broad as the notion of sustainability itself.

Three main categories of project development may be discerned in Higher Education institutions, namely:

- whole institutional business practices related to human and material resources procurement;
- whole institutional practices designed to raise awareness and conceptualize relevant aspects of day-to-day behaviour;
- whole institutional practices in terms of curriculum development, that is, content, technology and instructional approaches.

Of these the instructional approaches, especially those that may be used in interdisciplinary programmes, are most likely to produce and enhance sustainable development in the long term while, at the same time, facilitating the development of 'sustainability literacy'.

Sustainability literacy in higher education

Sustainability literacy can be regarded as the outcome of successful education for sustainable development, where the concepts and practicalities of sustainable development are understood, embedded and integrated into practice by the individual. As such it can be likened to other genres of literacy that have developed in the twenty-first century, such as computer literacy and scientific literacy (Colucci-Gray 2006). Described as the skills and attitudes needed to be a positive change agent for society (Rowe 2002), the rationale, as proposed in the 1987 Brundtland report and by the United Nations DESD 2005–2014, is that the need for radical change and action at international, national, institutional and individual levels can only be brought about by such sustainability literacy. Higher education has a key role to play in achieving this.

Murray and Murray (2007) note that much has been written on the need to embed sustainability and sustainable development in higher education, both in the curriculum and in institutional management. This is part of the national and international endorsement of the UN's DESD 2005–2014, and in turn justifies the need for a further rethink on sustainability literacy pedagogies. One of the main challenges for educational development within the higher education sector is grasping and applying the multidimensional nature of sustainable development in its business operations, scholarship and curriculum. It is argued that problems with the conceptualization of sustainable development pose a significant challenge for its integration into the curriculum (Murray and Murray 2007: 285; Roberts and Roberts 2007); conversely, Onwueme and Borsari (2007) observe that models that clarify the meaning and philosophy of sustainable development may encourage a popular culture of acceptance. Cortese proposes a solution via a change in attitude, using Einstein's observation that 'the significant problems we face cannot be solved at the same level of thinking we were at when we created them' (Cortese 1999: 9). Such a change in attitude is premised on the hypotheses that teachers and learners do not invariably have a positive attitude towards learning about ESD, and that both explicit and implicit dissonance are commonplace in terms of the application of knowledge about sustainable development to choices and actions.

Apart from this notion of dissonance, two issues have been raised in the literature with regard to the attributes of the substantive content of the curriculum in higher education institutions. First is the compartmentalization of the curriculum relating to sustainability. Cortese (1999) argues that though 'HEIs are significant leverage points that reflect and inform mindsets' they fail because 'a fundamental structural problem of the current educational system is the inclination to treat environmental education as yet another specialty, not unlike sociology, or biology' (Cortese 1999: 11). Such a treatment ignores the interdisciplinary approach that is instrumental in developing sustainability literacy. Second is the inclination to treat sustainable development as environmental education. This has been demonstrated in a recent

UK study by Murray and Murray (2007), which found that wider aspects of sustainability were not fully taken into consideration. In the United States, Clugston and Calder (1999) observed that in many programmes the emphasis is on environmental issues rather than sustainability. Four years later, in another survey, Clugston and Calder found that 11 per cent of US colleges taught Environmental Studies degrees, with 43 per cent offering minors in environmental or sustainability studies. However, the main concern remained the fact that 'these programmes are based in biology and chemistry departments and do not teach sustainable development; nor do they make integrated thinking and decision making an integral part of the approach' (Calder and Clugston 2003: 1010).

These analyses concur with that of Flint et al. (2000), who argue that skills in interdisciplinary teaching are fundamental for educators' competence to teach sustainability literacy in higher education. Such issues are central to creating feasible instructional strategies and Rowe (2002) has provided a broad range of models for integrating sustainability literacy into the higher education curriculum. However, these models are based on the assumption that students, planners and faculty within the higher education environment are invariably more resonant than dissonant about ESD which, as has already been demonstrated, is rarely the case. This problem might be addressed most effectively through instructional approaches that address the dissonant gap between knowledge and action. The fundamental argument here is that any proportion of dissonance about ESD is significant because it reduces the efficacy and success of sustainable development learning and teaching. It can, however, be addressed through pedagogical strategies that focus on attitudinal instruction.

Pedagogical strategies for attitudinal instruction

Although a substantial amount of work has been done on instructional strategies for sustainability literacy in higher education, for example by Rowe (2002), developing a set of appropriate pedagogies that can be applied to various programmes is still a challenge for practitioners. A recent survey by Cotton et al. (2007) found that a variety of pedagogies are deployed in sustainability literacy in higher education, including case studies and experiments

(Adomssent et al. 2007; Buchan et al. 2007; Sipos et al. 2008). The basis for these approaches is drawn from the work of Bloom and Krathwol (1956), who developed three overlapping 'domains', or categories of learning.

- The cognitive domain (or knowledge domain) relates to recalling, understanding, applying, analysing, synthesizing and evaluating the subject, object or data in a learning situation. In an attempt to simplify the complexity of sustainable development as a concept and in order to identify a pedagogy that reflects this model, Lourdel et al. (2007) developed what they describe as a cognitive map of student perceptions of sustainable development. Warburton's work (2003) also lays emphasis on the cognitive domain, developing a structure that organizes information into a coherent whole, with emphasis on the 'underlying meaning' (Warburton 2003: 45).
- The affective domain relates to receiving, responding to, valuing, organizing and internalizing the learning situation and, in so doing, developing appropriate behaviours consequent upon the learning. Shephard (2008) observes that although educators generally emphasize the cognitive domain in teaching and assessment, it is the affective domain that should be emphasized in ESD instructional design. This approach is also supported by Barth et al. (2007) who argue that ESD requires the development of a competency approach built around learners discovering and analysing their own value systems.
- The psychomotor domain relates to imitating, manipulating, developing precision, articulating related skills and naturalizing. The authors who advocate this approach use different specific pedagogic techniques. Murray and Murray (2007), for instance, hold that enquiry-based learning in ESD is instrumental in eliciting change of behaviour among learners. Flint et al. (2000) draw the notion of experiential learning from Dewey (1963) to argue that ESD should develop the competency of teachers to be able to act and plan 'seamlessly' in accordance with interdisciplinary programmes. The notion of experience is also employed in Domask (2007), but here the emphasis is on engagement and empowerment of students rather than the theory–practice oscillation.

'Bloom's taxonomy' (as it is often termed) was developed in the late 1950s and early 1960s, initially as a set of broad criteria for evaluating learning (Bloom and Krathwol 1956). However, further exploration of the concept proved that this taxonomy was also instrumental in pre-engagement (planning), engagement (the learning and teaching process) and post-engagement (assessment) (Martinez-Pons 2003). Most recent publications on the pedagogies that best suit ESD in higher education support the use of one of Bloom's categories. However, Kagawa (2007) specifically states that effective learning in ESD could be facilitated by both cognitive and affective domains as a means of taking action towards the students' preferred futures. Sipos et al., on the other hand, use all three elements of Bloom's taxonomy (interpreted as pertaining to knowledge, attitude and skills) to create a model of 'transformative sustainability learning', which relates to head, heart and hands (Sipos et al. 2008: 69).

In the light of these conceptual and theoretical approaches, it can be argued that an effective ESD pedagogy or instructional approach should be underpinned by all three elements of Bloom's taxonomy. It is however limiting to regard attitude as belonging exclusively to the affective domain; it has a broader meaning and role in instructional design, particularly as regards education for sustainable development.

Attitudinal instruction for sustainability literacy

The incorporation of attitudinal instruction into instructional design implies an attempt to embed attitude change, both in the teaching and learning objectives and the learning outcomes. One of the main theories widely used by social psychologists in relation to attitude change and persuasion is the Elaboration Likelihood Model developed in the late 1970s and early 1980s (Petty and Cacioppo 1981). Its main precept includes a number of key arguments about persuasion. When a persuasive message is presented, the receiver may choose either to evaluate its logical content (the central route) or to assess its credibility, attractiveness and the credentials of its source (the peripheral route). The central route is characterized by a greater level of analysis or elaboration, which in turn makes the persuasive effects of the message stronger. These arguments are based on extensive evidence drawn from numerous experiments and have been replicated by others, notably Bohner and Wänke (2002); O'Keefe (2002); and Erwin (2001). Rucker and Petty (2004) extend the concept by concluding that there is a correlation between the strength of an attitude and a counter-argument, irrespective of whether the latter is failed or successful (Rucker and Petty 2004). This implies that the overriding objective in developing an instructional model for ESD for higher education is to achieve the highest possible level of elaboration among students, faculty and planners.

Kamradt and Kamradt (1999) recognize the importance of elaboration in teaching and learning for sustainable development and provide a generic instructional design framework which is based on a detailed understanding of attitude. They define attitude as a 'psychological structure' that responds 'quickly and effectively to environmental situations related to the satisfaction of fundamental personal needs' (Kamradt and Kamradt 1999: 570). This implies that there is a relationship between the internal consistency in an attitude and personal needs or survival. Attitudinal dissonance, therefore, is a situation where this consistency fails to be perceived. Given that education for sustainable development is characterized by inconsistencies or dissonance, it appears that attitudinal instruction may restore internal consistency in the understanding and application of ESD. The implication is that *attitude* could be the focus for instruction. This is based on a specific conceptualization of the term, highlighted by Snelbecker:

> I have heard teachers and trainers complain that their students have *an attitude* as though an *attitude* is almost automatically 'bad'. Having 'an *attitude*' is an important goal of instruction. (Snelbecker 1999: 661)

This approach to the understanding and treatment of attitude is different from the looser use which refers exclusively to the affective aspect of learning (Seel and Dijkstra 2004). The instructional design which focuses on attitude, as proposed here, presupposes that an existing attitude may be characterized by dissonance with respect to change to a target attitude. A solution to this dissonance – or lack of internal consistency – is attitudinal instruction with a specific internal structure or components (Kamradt and Kamradt 1999).

According to Kamradt and Kamradt's (1999) model, the three learning domains of Bloom's taxonomy (affective, cognitive and psychomotor) represent components of attitude which are fundamental to learning. All three components interact to organize the thought process in accordance with the hierarchy of individual needs (Maslow 1943) and carry out an interactive process which characterizes the learner's thoughts during the introduction of a persuasion message. The affective domain signals the feelings attached to the idea or phenomenon, the cognitive domain examines alternatives and prioritizes, and the psychomotor domain deals with the feasibility of action. Kamradt and Kamradt (1999) argue that although there is a propensity to defend a particular attitude, mental and emotional energy may be afforded in repeated rounds of the same process until the resultant attitude meets needs.

Although this process is used subconsciously, questioning will elicit explicit answers related to the development of the attitude through the three components, for instance:

- how does the situation make you feel? (affective);
- what are your thoughts on it? (cognitive);
- why would you do what you are thinking? (psychomotor).

The answers to these questions are central to the transformation of attitudes. A logical integration of the three components aims at realizing internal consistency. When this happens there will be no remaining dissonance because the attitude will serve to resolve the individual's basic need. Should the process meet an inconsistency, the attempt to integrate the three domains will fail to resolve the particular need it is designed for and will again result in attitudinal dissonance.

Instructional strategy

Attitudinal instruction is an instructional strategy which focuses on identifying, activating and addressing attitudinal dissonance with a view to offering the option to produce consistency and achieving resonance. This process is dependent on the willingness of the receiver of the message (students, faculty and planners) to choose the central route described above, which allows a high level of elaboration and success in persuasion (Petty and Cacioppo 1981). According to Kamradt and Kamradt, attitudinal dissonance is subject to the 'principle of variable proportion' (1999: 571), where the proportion of application of the three components of attitude within a learning situation is not always equal. This variability is driven by the nature of the subject matter and by the attitudinal component preferences of the learner. Imbalances in proportion generate flawed instructional strategies, described by Kamradt and Kamradt (1999) as:

- the revival preacher who targets solely the affective component of the attitude (belief and behaviour are ignored);
- the debate champion who appeals only to the cognitive component (to the exclusion of the affective and behavioural aspects);
- the dictator who uses power to control behaviour.

The ultimate objective of attitudinal instruction is to obtain a balanced proportion of the three components in the learning process.

The following attitudinal instructional model may be used in instructional design in order to achieve a proportionate balance. The process is carried out through the identification of the initial attitude, followed by the intermediate attitude and the target attitude:

Activate current attitude
(create a situation that exposes the learner's attitude to the target attitude)

Diagnose the dissonant components
(by asking questions related to the affective, cognitive and behavioural domains)

Address the most dissonant component
(for affective dissonances use values and conditioning, for cognitive use persuasion, for psychomotor use demonstration and action)

Consolidate the intermediate attitude
(using explicit events to proceed to the target attitude)

Test to see how actionable the new attitude is

Transfer the new attitude into a relevant field of practice.

The model above could be designed to be adopted in various aspects of the curriculum content and delivery modes. The most specific approach would be to focus on all the components and embed them into the learning objective and outcomes by ensuring that the target attitudes are clearly delineated, the dissonant components are specifically identified and challenged and active learning is used to consolidate new attitudes. The general aim of instruction is identification, which means eliciting the highest possible level of elaboration and applying the persuasive message thereafter. The activation and diagnosis stages are a direct method for engaging the receivers (students, faculty and planners) in a central route of persuasion. This means setting the interaction up to involve all the counterarguments to both sustainability and sustainable development and thus to tackle inherent problems of dissonance that surround this topic.

Conclusion

Sustainability and sustainable development are complex and interrelated concepts that are of increasing importance in higher education across the world.

Achieving the goals of both sustainability and sustainable development is, however, beset with problems, many of which arise from the dissonance that surrounds both the key concepts and the concomitant behaviour required to realize appropriate outcomes. It can be seen therefore, that if sustainability and education for sustainable development are to be addressed effectively in higher education this must be done through fostering higher levels of sustainability literacy in order to challenge the attitudes which underpin the dissonance associated with sustainability. An appropriate instructional model to inform pedagogy will be required if such levels of sustainability literacy are to be achieved. As a greater international understanding of the concepts of sustainability and sustainable development emerges, it becomes increasingly important that a relevant model of learning and teaching in higher education is identified and deployed in order to address dissonance and ensure the effectiveness of sustainable development in education. It is argued here that two logically related theoretical foundations are proposed for developing such an instruction strategy, namely Bloom's taxonomy (Bloom and Krathwol 1956), and attitudinal instruction based on the work of Kamradt and Kamradt (1999). All the components of attitude in identified in Kamradt and Kamradt's (1999) model (cognitive, affective and psychomotor) will be required to present persuasive messages and counteract the inhibiting effects of dissonance. Testing and transferring imply developing assessment, projects and audit trails with respect to attitude.

This model will enable the attitudinal dissonance that underpins the dilemmas facing educators in making sustainability a popular culture for learners and teachers in higher education to be reconsidered and confronted. The use of attitudinal instruction may then be deployed as a means of developing attitudinal consistence among learners in higher education and hence resolving the problem of dissonance. It will also ensure that sustainability literacy can become a permanent concept that outlives the UN's Decade of Education for Sustainable Development. The application of this instructional approach adds to the raft of instructional strategies currently used for facilitating sustainability literacy and supporting both sustainability and sustainable development.

Part Two
Pedagogy and the Institutional Context

Part Two explores the ways in which some of the broad policy issues outlined in the first section are translated into procedures and practices at the institutional level. It focuses particularly on the shaping of the learning landscape through the pedagogies involved in the creation and transmission of knowledge, on the strategies deployed to enhance teaching and learning and on the increasing emphasis on the student as learner and use of technology in student learning. Each chapter, in considering different aspects of pedagogy within the institutional context, draws attention to the contested nature of policy, to the problems involved in responding positively to the evolving topology of the learning landscape and to the changing conceptualization of the proper function of the university.

Beckton considers some central aspects of the policy agenda, using the example of the work of EDUs in supporting both the creation and transmission of knowledge. He argues that the conceptualization of what a university is has moved from the traditional Humboldtian model to one based on the human capital needs of society as perceived by policy makers. He explores the extent to which EDUs can realistically meet demands for enhanced teaching quality within the requirements of the increasing instrumental policy context of higher education. Using case study data, he begins by examining how EDUs might contribute to quality assurance while balancing the demand for enhanced teaching quality with the requirements of an increasing instrumental higher educational environment and concludes that EDUs themselves must establish clear notions of sound professional practice based on the needs of their own institutions if they are to exert significance influence on teaching and learning.

Crawford provides a rare empirical study of continuing professional development (CPD) in higher education from the perspective of the academic staff of one university. She locates her analysis of the changes and continuities, tensions and complexities that surround the conceptualization and practice of continuing professional development in higher education within the current policy context established by the Dearing Report and, in particular, the establishment of the Higher Education Academy and the National Professional Standards for Teaching in Higher Education. She considers the different meanings attached to CPD, the differences in form and approach to what constitutes CPD activity, the relationship between policy and practice at an institutional level. She concludes by considering the gap between institutional and individual interests and expectations in CPD provision and argues that this gap must be addressed if CPD is to significantly influence teaching and learning in higher education.

Higher education institutions often see technology as a solution to many of the problems associated with teaching and learning. Watling argues that there is a danger that the internet might be considered as a disruptive technology within the learning landscape. While the internet is a powerful agent for change in education, many academic staff in universities are unfamiliar with the latest web developments. Thus, they may fail to recognize the possibilities that these developments offer, the diverse ways in which they may be used, their potential for having a profound effect on the learning landscape and their impact on the creation and transmission of knowledge. Taking the example of Web 2.0 applications, which she sees as being at the core of the online environment with which students are currently engaged, she argues that universities must seek to reduce this new digital divide, which is less about differential access to computers and more about differential skills that lead to unequal capacity to make the best use of such an environment.

Educational Development Units: The Challenge of Quality Enhancement in a Changing Environment

Julian Beckton

5

Introduction

Educational development units (EDUs) sometimes referred to as 'academic development units' can be defined as departments within universities that have been given a specific responsibility for improving the quality of learning and teaching in their host university. In recent years, since 2000, they have largely been funded through the provision of the Teaching Quality Enhancement Fund (TQEF), which has had two distinct effects. First, it has led to a rather pragmatic focus on the social, economic and institutional values that underpin educational policy rather than the more educational issues of academic freedom, professional autonomy and the search for knowledge noted by Stevenson and Bell, in Chapter 1 of this book. Second, as the TQEF is temporary and due to end in 2010, it has also put units under some pressure to search for a stronger intellectual basis for educational development, in order to ensure their own survival. It is argued here that this is linked to the notion of 'teaching quality enhancement'. The nature of exactly what constitutes teaching quality enhancement is not entirely clear however, and in fact there appear to be considerable differences in the roles that EDUs perform in different institutions.

Commonly, EDUs are involved in providing CPD for academic staff, but they may also be implementing national initiatives such as the introduction of personal development planning into the curriculum, or managing technological innovations, ranging from the management of an institutional VLE (Virtual Learning Environment) to providing advice on the use of a specific product, for example the Turnitin Plagiarism Detection Service. This extremely superficial summary hints at the complexity of the task EDUs face. The meaning of concepts such as 'teaching', 'learning' and 'quality' is still subject to some debate, and as Crawford points out in Chapter 6 of this volume, different academic disciplines take different approaches to teaching and learning. It follows that there are also likely to be different conceptions of what constitutes quality. Additionally, there is an external discourse of quality control, which argues that it is possible to measure the amount of development that takes place. In the sense that one can count the number of workshops delivered, the number of interactions between staff of the unit and academic staff, this is true. However that perception of truth rests on the simplistic implication that teaching is characterized as the transmission of knowledge from one mind to another, which contrasts with the conception of learning as occurring when students participate in and reflect on activities that promote learning as, for example, described in the work of Biggs (2003) and Laurillard (2002).

The author is currently conducting research into EDU staffs' perceptions of their role, and how far these relate to the structural and functional models of the university that can be found in the literature. Although this research is in its early stages it has involved visiting EDUs and interviewing the staff working in them; this chapter uses some of these findings and personal experience of working in an EDU to discuss how EDUs, given their relatively small size, might set about effecting significant change in a potentially risk-averse higher education environment. Lack of space precludes an extensive discussion of the relevance of the different models of the university, but the authors of other chapters have drawn attention to influences on higher education, for example Karran's discussion of the influence of the Humboldtian model of a research intensive university and Neary and Winn's discussion of the 'research-informed teaching' university will both be influential in informing the debate within and around EDUs. This chapter concentrates on the practical difficulties facing EDUs in what is currently a rather instrumental environment.

The complexity of the task facing EDUs is illustrated by the diversity of the units themselves. Gosling (2001) shows that there is a remarkable range of titles, organizational positions and to a lesser extent size of units. The titles of the units are quite revealing. The words 'learning and teaching' are included in the names of 43 per cent of the units surveyed. In the pre-1992 universities there was a high occurrence of the phrases 'staff development', 'quality enhancement' and 'academic development' or 'academic practice'. In a recently published update to his study, Gosling (2008) shows that this diversity has, if anything, increased. The title 'academic practice' is of interest because it clearly incorporates a focus on wider aspects of academic work than simply teaching. For example, as Blackmore and Blackwell (2006) pointed out, research and administration are usually regarded as an important part of the work of a university academic, yet are not often accorded the same attention as teaching by the research literature.

The type of university appears to have a strong influence over where in the institution EDUs are situated. In new universities, created after the Higher Education Act of 1992, they tend to be centrally located, perhaps being seen as an integral part of a more corporate management style. In pre-1992 universities, they tend to form part of larger administrative units such as quality offices, staff development or human resources departments. Although it is less usual, in the 2008 survey Gosling indicated that about 10 per cent of EDUs were attached to faculties. He also reported that heads of EDUs in the new universities were more likely to regard themselves as senior managers. This may be a reflection of the principal research method he chose to employ: a survey of heads of EDUs in the United Kingdom. In fact, he notes that relatively few of these heads chaired any major university committee. The perception of the EDU as belonging to the 'centre', that is the administrative centre of the university, rather than being associated with the more academic side of the university such as faculties, may have an important effect on its interaction with colleagues, and this issue is examined in some detail below.

If EDUs have anything in common with each other, it is that they tend to be small, although there are exceptions. Gosling (2001) reported that they typically had between one and eight staff, both academic and administrative. There also appear to be a high number of staff employed on fixed term contracts, often related to project funding, and a heavy dependence on part-time staff. Having said that, this kind of employment pattern is quite common in Higher Education generally (Sanders 2004), so it may not be reasonable to characterize it as typical of EDUs. Another factor in common is that they are often seen as a locus of technological innovation, although very few have any technical staff, in the sense of those with computer programming skills, or developers of educational technology. Indeed, as Watling notes in Chapter 7, internet developers are outstripping the support that institutions are able to provide and this places an obligation on EDUs not only to keep up to date with the technology but also to attempt to influence the pedagogical processes which the technology is designed to support. It is easy to conceive how units might become involved in innovations that use technology, but are not in themselves technological. An example of this is the use of the Turnitin

Plagiarism Detection Service. Here the development aim is to persuade colleagues to use the service to teach students about plagiarism by incorporating submission to Turnitin as part of the assessment regime, as opposed to simply using it *post facto* to catch malefactors. For further details of this approach see Carroll and Appleton (2001).

Contested ideas of the university

It is not only EDUs that are diverse. The idea of the university itself is contested, and this inevitably affects how EDUs are perceived both by themselves and by others. Views range from a rather pessimistic economic instrumentalism (Evans 2004) through ideas about training the mind (Newman 1853) and the Humboldtian 'research orientation' (UNESCO 2000) to Barnett's post modern 'supercomplex' institution (Barnett 2000); such diversity can challenge whether the university remains in any meaningful sense. Barnett points out that the university traditionally stood above the community it served, and as a result enjoyed a freedom not extended to other bodies in the wider society; this allowed it to explore universal themes of truth, knowledge, criticality and learning. However post-modern and post-structuralist philosophies suggest that no ontological position whatsoever can be taken with any credible authority, although as Barnett acknowledges, this kind of relativism is itself a position. The result is a world of 'proliferating and even mutually contesting frameworks, a world of supercomplexity' (Barnett 2005b: 789). In fact, although Barnett's analysis is valuable, one does need to acknowledge that the activities of the university are marked by certain dominant discourses, for example, gender, the world of work (and a very specific, corporate-oriented type of work at that), and disciplinary hegemony (Becher and Trowler 2001).

The concept of the university as an instrument of national economic development has gained some wider currency. Evidence for this can be seen in the growth of an increasing discourse of consumerism in higher education. At one end of the scale students increasingly see themselves as paying for a service, and they are less likely to accept either what they see as poorly delivered lectures in lecture rooms which are too small, equipped (if at all) with unreliable equipment, or problems in accessing tutors, library and computing services. At the other end of the scale, government ministers can hold a very narrow view of what higher education is for. The following quotation from Charles Clarke, a former Secretary of State for Education, is revealing:

> What I have said on a number of occasions . . . is that the mediaeval concept of the university as a community of scholars is only a very limited justification for the state to fund the apparatus of universities. It is the wider social and economic role of universities that justifies more significant state financial support. (quoted in Evans 2004: 43)

Thus the university is seen, from one perspective at least, as having a clear function with regard to the wider economic environment in which it operates. The purpose of higher education is to provide skilled graduates who will work to promote the economic well-being of the nation. The implication for the EDU is that it should be developing teachers who are best placed to teach to that end.

This places the EDU in a difficult position. It is not usually a significant income generator in itself, which can put it under pressure to justify the funding that it receives. There is a need to do more than promote a debate about what constitutes good practice, or efficient teaching. In short, the EDU needs to provide evidence of its activity, and demonstrate that such activity is effective and of value both to the university and to the wider higher education community. An EDU cannot ignore external demands for accountability. The challenge is to balance the normative external pressures on the institution from policy makers, fund holders and other stakeholders with the need to encourage a reflective, exploratory ethos that will engage teaching colleagues, and in doing so make a convincing case for its continuing existence. To some extent, this depends on the context in which the EDU is operating.

The complexity of university teaching and the place of the EDU

An important concern of EDUs, perhaps the most important, is the improvement of practices related to teaching. Teaching however is underpinned by many different values and, as Stevenson and Bell note in Chapter 1, these values are just as often economic, social and institutional as they are educational. This diversity, along with the multiplicity of conceptions of the university, is reflected in many different approaches to teaching. As Scott (2005) puts it, the concept of teaching is becoming somewhat disjointed. First there is a proliferation of new courses and disciplines emerging. Second, there is an increase in the diversity of delivery methods and a growth in part-time, flexible and on-line learning. Third, there has been a growth in the use of virtual learning environments (VLEs) and other applications that make use of technology. Finally, there has been a shift from teaching to learning, meaning that the teacher is less important in the totality of the student's learning experience. Libraries, databases and pastoral support all play an increasingly important role. Clearly Scott's arguments render the model of teaching as transmission unsustainable, but in some respects he doesn't go far enough. As Westera (2004) reminds us:

> Technological innovation is often seen as a straightforward process of improvement – actually it is a diverse and complex field of action. It concerns a mix of new developments in pedagogy and technology, it implies changes at organisational level and it touches on fundamental concepts like progress, change, control, functionality, anticipation, mediation, acceptation etc. (Westera 2004: 502)

EDUs, then, need to do far more than simply concentrate on improving teaching. Technology in particular is associated with a range of normative requirements (in many polities often mandated by legislation) such as usability, IPR management, and data protection. The implication for an EDU is that it needs to develop its own philosophy around what constitutes good teaching which may not, indeed probably does not, match the philosophy of teaching held within the different departments. In parallel (it is implied) the EDU needs to develop a rather deontic model of appropriate professional practice, especially around technology.

The implication of the existence of the TQEF is that there exists a normative set of rules about what constitutes good teaching, and that EDUs are the logical repository of some form of privileged access to those rules. Faculties appear to want to distance themselves from that idea, possibly because they represent a threat to what they see as their freedom to teach in the most appropriate way. Clegg (2003a) for example, in her case study of a single institution, draws attention to the attitude of an interviewee:

> He designated the [Learning Teaching and Assessment] co-ordinator role (i.e. his own) as being the [Learning and Teaching Institute] (the central educational development unit) person in order to distance it from his own School identity. (Clegg 2003a: 809)

This seems to be a very revealing observation showing that for many teaching staff, even if they have a formal educational development role, the EDU is still not seen as part of the major academic enterprise. Essentially it is part of the 'centre', and as such is still seen as external to the work of the individual departments: 'The idea of the pragmatic emerged through a series of dualities, all of which asserted the significance of local practical wisdom as against policy and theoretical knowledge in the centre' (Clegg 2003a: 810).

Clegg's case study was not about EDUs as such, but those who work in EDUs will have little difficulty in recognizing the dualities to which she refers. On the one hand there is the disciplinary knowledge which is, for the most part, what attracted academic staff to the profession in the first place and on the other there is the encompassing regulatory framework, whose importance is recognized by academic staff, but which they do not always prioritize.

Tight (2003) has convincingly demonstrated that academic staff are highly educated professionals with a great deal of independence who can display considerable ingenuity in continuing to work to their preferred style, while superficially accepting change. Sharpe (2004) draws on generic notions of professional development to argue that while there may be a set of basic competences involved in university teaching a large proportion of what higher education professionals do is implicit – in other words, they find it very difficult to describe their work. Here there is an echo of the reflective practitioner (Schön 1995), but although Sharpe concedes that reflection is a valuable learning activity, she suggests that it is not adequate to explain professional development. Theories of personal reflection do not sit easily with, for example, concepts of social learning and the need to articulate, in Schön's phrase, the 'professional artistry' of university teachers; neither is reflection particularly helpful in making that artistry available to others.

There is some truth in this, but it seems to underplay the value of tacit knowledge. Tacit knowledge is valuable precisely because it is tacit and so can be adapted to different situations. If tacit knowledge is articulated there is a strong risk of it being converted into a more or less rigid set of rules which, if not discouraging reflection entirely, lessens the likelihood that it will occur. This is not an argument that academics should not attempt to articulate their tacit knowledge in their teaching. Clearly education would be a challenging business if no one articulated what they knew! Rather it is an argument that the ability to respond to different situations is a requirement for anyone who works in the modern university. An EDU that sees its primary role as simply training, or the application of what are sometimes called technical-rational solutions, is unlikely to succeed in engaging with colleagues who will not recognize the experience of others, or any proposed solutions, as being relevant to their own practice unless there is a properly critical debate about the problem.

Gosling (2001) was clear that the role of the EDU is predominantly to encourage reflection. He states that the purpose of these units is

> to create an environment in which debate can flourish about what constitutes good practice and how that may vary across different contexts and for different types of students. Learning is not simply more or less effective and teaching is not simply more or less efficient, nor can good practice simply be disseminated.
> (Gosling 2001: 75)

While this is unlikely to appeal to those who view the university as an instrument of national economic development and seek to measure its performance in meeting that end, it does support the argument that educational development needs to take greater account of the situated nature of learning. The argument here is that learning can indeed be more effective, teaching can be more efficient and good practice can be disseminated: educational development is based on these precepts, while acknowledging that the task is both difficult and complex.

Given this complexity, it is not entirely surprising to discover that EDUs adopt a variety of strategies to bring about the objective of enhancing the quality of teaching in their host universities. What is emerging from the case studies collected in the course of the current research is a clear emphasis on the development of academic staff, rather than a concern for the development of learning materials or the production of normative guidelines about, for example, how technology should be used to meet the needs of specific groups of students.

EDU practices

Given the multiplicity of demands placed upon them and the relative lack of clarity about what is expected of them, it is not perhaps surprising to find that EDUs offer a wide variety of services. These might include provision of a staff development programme, the provision and administration of awards for teaching, the evaluation of new technologies, the provision of accredited programmes such as postgraduate diplomas in higher education, masters or doctoral courses, help-desk type services for VLEs, the writing of bids for external funding, or the implementation of specific incentives, such as the introduction of personal development planning into the curriculum. There is no space here for a full discussion of these, but the use of new technologies to promote learning is discussed in more detail, because it is something that most EDUs appear to be involved in.

The promotion of technological tools to enhance learning is sometimes criticized as making no significant difference to teaching and learning, but there is a counter argument that teachers are not, in general, using technology to do anything significantly different in terms of the pedagogical approach they are taking. For example, there is little difference in pedagogical terms between writing on a blackboard, using overhead projector slides or using PowerPoint software. Garrison and Anderson (2003), for example, argue for the use of asynchronous discussion groups to allow the teacher to engage more directly with the different experiences that students bring to the learning sessions, broaden the coverage of a teaching session and increase student engagement. As a respondent in one of the author's case studies put it:

> You have to go into a discussion group, post a comment, or something. For example, there's one where you have to read two or three pieces of literature which you find and review them and post them on line with a comment about why people should look at it, and then you have to go to somebody else's and look at what they've said and post a response to them, and then somebody posts a response to you, and you post a response to that, and you have to do that online. You can't do it otherwise. (Case Study 1, Respondent 2)

The implication here is that technology is necessary for this particular EDU to successfully deliver quality enhancement. The unit's students (who are really teachers) appear not to relish discussing the two or three pieces of literature in the more conventional way that they might expect their own undergraduates to – that is, by participating in a tutorial where people are physically present. Instead the technology of the asynchronous discussion group is needed to get them to communicate across the whole group. Even if the members of a seminar group are present in the same room, it is rare for the traditional model to allow time for the full consideration to what each member of the group has said. There is no sense here that the EDU is prescribing a teaching technique, but it is not unreasonable that teachers exposed to this type of development may begin to explore this kind of approach with their own undergraduate students. The fact that this is described by the participant as 'some kind of assessment task', does however, rather imply that this is something that is not undertaken voluntarily by developing teachers and that its value is not immediately apparent to those participating in it.

Implicit in the previous paragraph is that EDUs may actually be more effective if they bring about enhancement surreptitiously. This is related to the argument above about the value of tacit knowledge. There is an acknowledgement of the constructivist idea that learners bring unique experience to the learning situation and the educational developer's job is not to tell learners what to do but to help them develop constructs, or ways of understanding or interacting with the world, that will fit into their own practice. Yet while surreptitiousness may be effective, it is not always of value in a target-driven organization, where accountability is regarded as particularly valuable.

There is however a second aspect to technological innovation more closely related to Sharpe's (2004) notion of competences. Before one can innovate with technology, one has to be able to use it. It is difficult to be specific about what it is reasonable to expect people to be able to do with technology in order to function effectively as a university teacher. While it appears rare for EDUs to offer entry level courses in technology, it is more common for them to offer workshops on those technologies that claim to have been designed for the support of teaching and learning: most obviously VLEs such as Blackboard, Web CT and Moodle. The University of Lincoln, for example, is in the process of switching to Blackboard from a long established system which staff were very familiar with. Here, the role of EDU staff was not primarily to deliver orientation workshops, which is largely being done by an external consultant, but to manage pilot programmes by offering one to one 'help-desk' type support for those involved in these programmes and conducting evaluations of them. EDU staff were also heavily involved in the project planning for the wider roll out of Blackboard across the university.

The focus on these technologies in the EDUs studied is very much on pedagogical rather than technological innovation. Staff in EDUs already seem to expect their academic colleagues to possess basic competences in using information technology. There is some justification for this, as technology has become almost ubiquitous in the modern workplace, but it may not be entirely warranted. There do remain staff who find technology slightly intimidating and this raises the question of how far an EDU should endeavour to raise the technical competency level of colleagues. It can of course be argued that this competence will come about through the process of engaging at a higher level with technology. Certainly, a constructivist pedagogical philosophy would hold that staff would develop their own individual ways of dealing with the practical requirements of technology, through reflection on their experiences of using it.

Conclusion

The aim of this chapter was to begin to explore the question of whether EDUs could realistically meet demands for enhanced teaching quality with the requirements of a rather instrumentalist higher education environment. The argument has been made that it is essential that educational developers work with the faculties, which means that they cannot realistically present themselves as loci of teaching expertise. Even if teaching practices within faculties occasionally leave something to be desired, practitioners are unlikely to respond well to corrective measures that originate outside their own disciplines, no matter how much academic theory informs those initiatives.

Having said that, the world is changing, most notably through rapid advances in technology and continuing government initiatives; these changes will happen whether those in universities like them or not. It can be argued that the variety of demands that are made on EDUs does render those working in them particularly well placed to handle these changes, through the adoption a more reflective approach to teaching development. Essentially this can be summarized as a belief that professionals (including university teachers) are able, through detailed and continuous scrutiny of their daily practice, to recognize what they are doing well, and why they are doing it well. Equally, they can recognize and develop what needs to be enhanced. This argues for a model of educational development of staff through a process of reward and recognition, such as using teaching portfolios to assess suitability for promotion, combined with the judicious use of funding to promote small innovative project work that delivers objectives that staff want to bring about in their teaching. While one cannot reasonably make large scale generalizations from small scale case studies there is no evidence that EDUs are attempting to impose a normative model of good teaching on academic colleagues.

As far as the technological enhancement of learning is concerned, it is possible to accuse EDUs of being rather reactive. There appears to be a focus on delivering workshops on technologies that staff are going to need in their work, for example in response to the roll-out of an institutional VLE. A more proactive approach might be to anticipate what technologies staff will need to use and provide support for that. This strategy does run the considerable risk that a lot of effort will be devoted to something that may never be needed, and which in any case will reach very few staff, as they will not attend workshops that they see as being of little value to their professional practice. All of this points to a conclusion that an EDU is apt to be far more successful if it works with academic colleagues to help them enhance their skills of reflection in the context of their own practice, rather than attempting to impose a set of externally derived quality criteria on them.

This has been a limited investigation into the role of the EDU in the modern university. There is a need for more research into the different aspects of its practice. Surveys of the extent to which academic staff engage with the services of units, and into the understandings that they hold of the EDU would be of great assistance in helping units to focus their services on the needs of teaching colleagues. A series of international case studies to compare the approaches taken to pedagogical innovation in different regulatory environments would also be of value. There is also a need for research into matters that space has precluded here, in particular collaboration between EDUs in different universities, the extent to which units produce learning materials for colleagues in the disciplines, what roles the EDU might play in bidding for funding for external projects, how the EDU relates to academic support services such as library, student welfare and computer services departments, and finally, into the emerging profession of 'educational developer'.

For the moment, the evidence from the case studies supports the argument that a successful EDU will be one that concentrates on building a learning environment appropriate to its host university, and which is pragmatic about helping staff to progress their careers in that university, rather than one which pays a disproportionate amount of attention to externally imposed targets. That is not to say that such targets should be ignored. Rather, the unit needs to seek agreement on how those targets should be interpreted in the context of its own university, and seek to meet them in a way that matches the range of working patterns in that institution. In fact, to do otherwise may well run the risk of failing to meet such targets. In short the EDU needs to be as much about research, especially into its own institution, as it is about development. Attempts to impose any prescriptive formula based on one idea of good teaching, even if that is based on sound pedagogical research, seem unlikely to succeed. In fact, given the wide variety of demands placed upon them, staff working in EDUs seem particularly well placed to handle the rapidly changing environment that is likely to characterize the twenty-first century higher education environment, provided of course that they follow their own advice and reflect extensively on their own practice.

Continuing Professional Development in Higher Education: Tensions and Debates in a Changing Environment

6

Karin Crawford

Introduction

It has been acknowledged that 'staff expertise is the most important asset in a university; without it literally nothing can be achieved' (Blackmore and Blackwell 2003: 23), yet the CPD of academics can be seen to take place within a complex array of competing challenges and perspectives. The nature of the academic role and the responsibilities attributed it are changing, along with the relationships to other roles both within and without the institution (Blackmore and Blackwell 2003). Added to this there are new national policy standards, requirements and budgetary barriers/drivers that may impact upon the institution and its members in different ways. The ways in which these factors, in a complex and changing context, might influence the behaviours and attitudes of academic staff towards CPD has been unclear. This chapter reports on qualitative data collected as one element of a larger research project that set out to increase understanding of influences on the CPD practices of academics. By first exploring some of the pertinent debates in the literature and following this with the experiences and practice of academics, as reflected in the research data, the chapter provides evidence of significantly contrasting perspectives on the issues. Through this research, three interconnected areas of potential tension and debate are highlighted: issues related to the definition and meaning attributed to CPD; differences in the form and approach to what constitutes CPD activity; and policy implementation.

It has been argued that 'top down institutional and quality agendas shape the context for much CPD' (Clegg 2003b: 42). In contrast however, the

Table 6.1 Key Demographics of Academic Research Participants

Pseudonym	Gender	Subject area	Is required to comply with a subject related professional CPD framework	Contractual tenure	Contracted working hours	Length of experience as an academic
Adam	M	Applied	No	Temporary	Hourly paid	6–10 years
Amanda	F	Applied	No	Fixed Term	Fractional	21 years+
Annie	F	Applied	No	Permanent	Full time	21 years+
Carla	F	Applied	Yes	Permanent	Full time	1–5 years
Catriona	F	Applied	No	Permanent	Full time	11–15 years
Chantrea	F	Pure	No	Temporary	Hourly paid	Under 1 year
Colin	M	Applied	No	Permanent	Part time	6–10 years
Elizabeth	F	Pure	No	Fixed Term	Full time	1–5 years
Honor	F	Applied	No	Fixed Term	Full time	1–5 years
Jameel	M	Applied	No	Permanent	Full time	1–5 years
Mike	M	Applied	No	Fixed Term	Hourly paid	1–5 years
Pascal	M	Applied	Yes	Permanent	Full time	6–10 years
Peter	M	Pure	No	Permanent	Full time	11–15 years
Ratana	F	Applied	No	Permanent	Full time	16–20 years
Rebecca	F	Applied	Yes	Permanent	Full time	6–10 years
Rhys	M	Applied	No	Permanent	Full time	Under 1 year

current research is underpinned by the view that to develop a meaningful understanding of CPD practices in academia it is necessary to start with an exploration of what academics understand by CPD, what they do, and why, taking account of the context within which it happens:

> [I]t is equally . . . important for the continuance of the university as we know it that we look systematically and critically at our own professional behaviour, at our structures of university self-governance, at our processes for peer review and at our underlying academic beliefs. (Dill 2005: 178)

These academic beliefs with regard to CPD have been little researched, hence the value of this project. To ascertain perceptions, qualitative interviews with a range of academics and managers were undertaken during the academic year 2007–2008, within one 'new' English university – that is, an institution granted university status since the 1992 Further and Higher Education Act. A total of 16 academics from across the institution were interviewed; the range of demographic profiles is given in Table 6.1. Five key informants were also interviewed: managers, staff directly involved in the professional development of academic staff and those who have responsibility for the enhancement of teaching and learning in the institution. With regard to the interviews with academics, a theoretical sampling approach was developed to reflect the aims and purposes of the research, ensuring the participation of those 'who might know' and enabling 'a cross-fertilization between these different interpretative currents' (Pawson and Tilley 1997: 160–1).

Political and academic debates

The research was both timely and pertinent, given the context of change in higher education and current debates about CPD within this context. In 1997 the UK government commissioned a study of higher education, to report with 'recommendations on how the purposes, shape, structure, size and funding of higher education . . . should develop . . . over the next 20 years' (NCIHE 1997: 3). This report, known as the Dearing Report after its chairman, continues to be influential today. However, its recommendations have been criticized for proposing 'a series of uneasy compromises between market forces, state control and professional interests' (Tapper and Salter 1998: 33) in the higher education sector. Further evidence of managerialism in the context of higher education can be found in the more recent government White Paper

The Future of Higher Education wherein, among a rhetoric of more freedom and self-determination for universities, examples are apparent of a furthering of the new managerialist discourse of 'recognition and reward'; 'quality and standards systems'; competition; and economic efficiency (DfES 2003: 50–1). Within this, despite the breadth and complexity of the academic role, this White Paper develops a focus on the enhancement of teaching. Illustrative of these approaches is the increasing focus on '. . . good-quality teaching for everyone . . .' by '. . . staff that are trained to teach and continue to develop professionally . . .' (DfES 2003: 49). Accordingly, the Higher Education Academy (HEA), which was created following the publication of the White Paper, developed the *United Kingdom Professional Standards Framework for teaching and supporting learning in higher education* (HEA 2006), hereafter referred to as the *Professional Standards Framework*. These standards aim to act as 'an enabling mechanism to support the professional development of staff engaged in supporting learning' with the underpinning areas of activity including the 'evaluation of practice and continuing professional development' and the professional value of a 'commitment to continuing professional development and evaluation of practice' (HEA 2006). To support the implementation of these standards, the Academy has development a non-mandatory individual professional recognition scheme and, more recently, an accreditation process for CPD frameworks within institutions.

Despite these drivers, the concept of CPD in academia is problematic, with further ambiguity arising from a range of alternative terms, which may have similar meanings, being in use in different settings at different times (Blackwell and Blackmore 2003a). In her theoretical meta-analysis of CPD in higher education, Clegg argues that 'the problem of CPD . . . of professionals in higher education is that it operates around a series of unresolved tensions' and goes on to describe 'fault lines in conceptualising' CPD (Clegg 2003b: 37). Notwithstanding an increasing focus on the CPD of academics, the Higher Education Academy's website, www.heacademy.ac.uk, does not include a definition of the concept. However, the Chartered Institute of Personnel and Development (CIPD) defines CPD as being 'a combination of approaches, ideas and techniques that will help you manage your own learning and growth' (www.cipd.co.uk). Clegg (2003b) argues that there are two 'dualisms' in respect of what is considered appropriate content and focus of CPD in higher education which reflect characteristic influences on academic identity. These are the research-teaching nexus and the tension between loyalties to the subject discipline and the organization.

There has been much written about the first of these, focusing on the differential status and importance afforded to research and teaching within universities (Barnett 2005c) leading to the emergence of 'two academic tribes – those who prioritize research . . . and those who tend to prioritize teaching' (Ramsden 1998, cited in Trigwell and Shale 2004: 523). This has consequent implications for the interpretation and impetus of CPD in the institution: strategically driven, formal development activities are commonly focused on teaching and learning, while activity that develops research and subject-related skills and knowledge is not so readily framed as CPD (Clegg 2003b). This is potentially further complicated by the *Professional Standards Framework* (HEA 2006). Traditionally academics were seen to engage in teaching, research and administration; however, the reality is that the 'academic role is in flux' (Blackmore and Blackwell 2003: 19) and can include a wider range of tasks and responsibilities. The *Professional Standards Framework* can be seen to have a focus on teaching and learning and may not, therefore, enable academics and institutions to take a more inclusive approach to considering CPD.

The second of Clegg's dualisms refers to a perceived tension between the potentially competing approaches and needs of the discipline and the institution. It has been argued that some academics may only give credence to, and prioritize, development opportunities created and offered from within their own discipline, where they may have the most interest and confidence, as opposed to enhancing their skills and knowledge in teaching (Zuber-Skerritt 1992; Allan et al. 2003). To understand influences on CPD at individual and institutional levels it is necessary to take account of these debates, along with the significantly varied approaches that different academic disciplines have to CPD (Clegg 2003b). These differences can be seen as evolving from epistemological sources with academics being positioned within many systems or communities, each of which may have different discourses, approaches to teaching and learning, understandings of CPD and priorities. In addition to inconsistencies related to the meanings attributed to CPD there is clear variance about the appropriate form and approach to CPD activity. The core of the issue can be seen to pivot on whether or not CPD activity is inclusive of formal and informal approaches to learning in the workplace.

Taking the metaphor of an iceberg, Knight (2006) argues that there is more tacit, contextual, situated knowledge below the surface, than there is formal, tangible and explicit knowledge above it, yet there is 'a tendency to regard professional or staff development as comprising only those sorts of activities that are formally recognised' (Clegg 2003b: 37). However, it is argued that the dichotomous distinction between formal and informal workplace learning is not helpful, as workplace learning is, in reality, an 'engagement in goal-directed activities that are structured by workplace experiences' (Billett 2002: 58). It is, however, important to consider the influence and expectations arising from the contemporary culture of higher education, where there is a perceived 'shift in the focus of higher education from a collegial to a managerial model' (D'Andrea and Gosling 2005: 18). It can be seen, for example, that both the *Professional Standards Framework* (HEA 2006) and institutional audit requirements may increase the value of professional development that is synonymous with formal approaches, such as accredited courses and training events. Consequently there is concern that requirements and regulations can result in CPD being 'accountancy-driven' and as such, development that cannot be scrutinized, evidenced and 'counted' will not be valued (Schuller and Field 2002). McWilliam (2002) adds to the voices of concern in raising disquiet about the standardization of professional development in a context that is valued for its ability to question and challenge. In a similar vein, Karran considers professional development within the context of academic freedom within Chapter 2 of this book. The complexity of 'measurability' and demands for evidence are seen to result in only two opposing potential solutions: high levels of trust, or strong regulation (Field 2002). Similarly Cullingford (2002) argues that mistrust is an insidious theme of current accountability agendas. Realistically, this may be a debate that has yet to fully surface in higher education. For example, the recently established process of HEA accreditation of institutional CPD frameworks could be seen to represent a process of devolution that supports institutional autonomy, or it could be argued that the perceived need for accreditation represents, in itself, reducing levels of trust.

A further area of potential tension and debate centres on the relationship between policy, implementation, institutional and individual interests. In a critique of broader lifelong learning policies, Field (2002: 201) conveys concern about the effectiveness of policy implementation, describing disparity between 'policy rhetoric and policy achievement' and 'conception and delivery'. With regard to CPD in academia, this may be partially explained by the apparent lack of consensus on the meaning and scope of the concept, which was discussed earlier. The CIPD definition cited earlier appears to focus on the individual, yet the literature shows that CPD in academia is increasingly led and informed by strategic objectives, managerial and institutional agendas (Blackmore and Blackwell, 2003; Clegg 2003b;). Thus 'the core tension in this relationship is that between those needs for the continuity of the work practice and individuals' needs to realise their personal or vocational goals' (Billett 2002: 56). Conversely, Zuber-Skerritt suggests that this relationship is situated in mutually influential social processes, in that: 'To change people means to create a different climate for generating different working relationships. Changed people are the result of changed climates, and changed climates are the results of changed people' (Zuber-Skerritt 1992: 158).

With regard to the institutional context of CPD, it can be seen that there are competing views about whose goals and needs should be the focus of relevant strategies. Citing the work of Land (2001), Clegg (2003b: 38) develops a distinction between 'domesticating tendencies' and 'critique', where the former aims to align CPD to the needs of the institution, and the latter has a more 'emancipatory purpose'. While overtly favouring critique and indicating concern about processes of CDP being 'enmeshed with the reform quality agenda', Clegg concedes that institutional agendas can be more inclusive and less discriminatory than forms of professional development that centre on exclusive networking (Clegg 2003b: 45). Blackwell and Blackmore (2003b) take this further and argue that the emphasis of any CPD strategy should be on institutional and departmental alignment and away from a focus on individual academics. However, despite some acknowledgement in the literature of the strengths of institutionally-led approaches, alternative approaches are advocated. For example, it is suggested that while professional development is a strategic activity, it is located in 'distributed activity systems' ensuring alignment to context within collaborative working environments (Knight 2006). Taking this further, Clegg develops the concept of 'making the academic department the hub of activities' (Knight and Trowler 2001, cited in Clegg 2003b: 47). However, there is some broad agreement in the literature that suggests that this debate, in reality, centres on a false dichotomy with both the institution and the individual potentially gaining from development activities to differing extents (Zuber-Skerritt 1992; Blackwell and Blackmore 2003b; Clegg 2003b).

The following sections of this chapter draw upon the research findings to explore three specific areas of potential tension and debate in respect of CPD in higher education. In particular, the discussion that follows demonstrates that the research findings, while supporting some of the assertions in the literature, more manifestly serve to highlight a number of significant disparities between the theoretical analysis and the reality of practice. The research can be seen, therefore to further 'problematise' the concept of CPD in higher education, acknowledging the complexities and encouraging on-going participative debate (Clegg 2003b).

The CPD debates in practice: defining CPD

The academics who participated in this study were each asked to articulate their understanding of CPD in the context of their practice. The responses provide evidence of the problematic nature of the concept as debated in the literature and of the additional challenge caused by a range of terms being used to convey similar notions, such as: staff development, educational development, self-development, lifelong learning and critical professional learning. More starkly apparent was that many of the participants had not previously given any thought to CPD and therefore the notion was essentially alien to them. This was in part explained by some of the academics as being due to professional development being embedded as an integral element to their daily work.

> I don't see it as being separate so I think . . . to me its almost like saying, do you eat and drink, do you actively eat and drink, in that I don't separate it very easily from day to day activities. (Carla)

This participant furthered the food metaphor to explain how she was having difficulty in conceptualizing CPD as an individual entity:

> It is like saying here's a pizza, but actually I don't want you to put the pizza together, what I want you to do is put the flour over there and the tomatoes there and the cheese there and the anchovies there . . . they only want you to see that bit, the pizza is the whole not just the ingredients in piles that you can pick and choose when you want to . . . I just see it as being part of my normal [daily work]. (Carla)

In the previous chapter, Beckton explored the possible implicit nature of some aspects of the academic role, particularly teaching, and the potential challenges this may have for collegiate, critical dialogue and social learning. Interestingly, the embedded and potentially hidden nature of professional learning that is expressed in this research, particularly in respect of subject specific development, appears to result in some academics perceiving CPD as being those areas of learning that lie outside their daily working practices. Thus Honor describes CPD as being '. . . developing skills that you don't develop through teaching or that are outside of your own subject area but they are things that you need to do, so like computing training for when you have to do administrative tasks'. Conversely, some of those interviewed described professional development as being that 'which enables practitioners or academics or teachers to fulfil their day job . . . to keep themselves up to date . . .' (Rebecca).

Others reflected on the complexity of the term, particularly in conceptualizing CPD within the context of working in a learning environment:

> It's about environments, context, professional environment context, I think it's a very multi-layered, multi-dimensional community of learning that's available for all of us and I think, actually, one of the things that working at the Uni does give you access to is that learning environment. (Colin)

When asked about whether, at the level of the institution, there was an agreed understanding of what was meant by CPD for academics, the key informants interviewed all felt that while there was implicit agreement about the benefits of CPD, it would not be possible to identify an agreed, recorded definition for the concept across the institution.

Many academics also articulated their awareness and experiences of the tensions caused by the disparity in perceived status and reward afforded to activities related to teaching and research (Clegg 2003b; Trigwell and Shale 2004; Barnett 2005c). Ratana, who describes the focus and enjoyment in her work as being 'around the teaching of students', expresses some frustration as she perceives that:

> As far as professional development within my subject is concerned, the way it is seen by my department is, it's all about your Ph.D. specialism, your research activity, your research group activity, your publication record, that is what they're all about, and really not a lot of commitment to the pedagogy principle, I don't think. (Ratana)

The challenge of dual professionalism was raised by many of the academic participants, with some individuals describing ways in which they work to 'integrate two professional disciplines, being for example a professional teacher and a professional manager' (Carla) and endeavouring to 'keep myself up to date with . . . teaching and learning techniques but also with my subject and developments in practice' (Catriona). The findings of the research data in this respect can be seen to contradict some of the theoretical assertions discussed earlier. As shown, some academics describe the challenges of pursuing pedagogically-related development, yet the literature suggests that institutionally CPD centres on knowledge and skills related to teaching and learning (Clegg 2003b), with further support for teaching and learning related CPD offered by the *Professional Standards Framework* (HEA 2006) and recognition of professional status through fellowship of the Higher Education Academy.

It is apparent that for many staff, as discussed by Allan et al. (2003), it is the developmental needs related to their subject and academic discipline that are most often prioritized. This may be partly due to the complex, dynamic and pressured academic role and personal career development pathways, rather than representing any intentional avoidance of other aspects of the academic role or indeed institution-wide priorities. When interviewed, Peter explained that:

> The bulk of my work is teaching . . . I have a fair dollop of administration, I am programme leader . . . and sit on various other committees . . . and then research comes at the end of it all. (Peter)

When asked about his CPD activities, however, Peter was very clear that he considered himself to be 'CPD active', explaining this was

> Because I'm learning new things all the time, I'm learning new statistical techniques, I'm learning new experimental techniques, I'm learning how to write, I'm learning how to take a subject area and pick out the bits that are going to lead to good publications . . . the bits that are going to move the theory of the discipline forward. (Peter)

Thus from this example, while Peter is embedded in the whole range of academic responsibilities, professional development can be seen to have been firmly focused on his discipline. An appreciation of these tensions was also evident from the key informants interviewed, one of whom explained that university lecturers perceive themselves principally as experts in their subject area and that this perception is reinforced by the students that they work with. With what she called a 'wariness' of 'cultivating the idea that people have a second professional identity as a teacher of their subject', one key informant stated that she appealed to colleagues as 'teachers of history, or teachers of forensic science', in order to attempt to recognize the whole of the academic role and emphasize that teaching and learning of subjects is one element of CPD activity for academic staff.

The CPD debates in practice: approaches to CPD

The significance of subject-related CPD is also apparent when academics describe the different activities which they perceive as contributing to their professional development. Most commonly these include formalized education and training opportunities, alongside informal learning. Within this, however, the interviews provide evidence of the truth of Knight's (2006) iceberg metaphor in that many of the professional disciplinary scholarship activities described represent informal development and learning, which is not always identified by individuals or institutions in terms of CPD.

> It doesn't really stop, you know, whether you are talking about individual students which everybody does, you know, we've got a problem here or this is great or whatever or you are talking about methodology, you think, am I talking about it or shall we have a meeting about it, you just do it. (Amanda)

It is also apparent from the data that many academics place great importance on learning and development through networking. Most commonly this is with colleagues based in other institutions nationally and internationally but, importantly, working in similar subject specialisms. Many interviewees expressed engagement in learning communities 'where the community practises the scholastic processes of conversation, involvement and engagement as modes of revealing knowledge' (Gibbs et al. 2004).

> I think that the learning takes place across a broad community which might be local, regional, national or international, so although we locate ourselves in institutions, I think if we swear allegiance to the institution too much, it will stop us all from learning and the real learning takes place when you get to the outside. (Colin)

When talking about approaches to CPD, the academics interviewed raised concern about it being one of many demands on their time, within an overall environment of 'ever increasing external demands placed upon institutions and individuals' (Cullingford 2002: 223). The National Student Survey (www.hefce.ac.uk/learning/nss), which is explored further by Hagyard in Chapter 9, is one example of such demands. In her interview, Elizabeth describes the 'backlash' from this survey with unexpected management directives about what was to be taught, leading to 'a real issue of quality of life' for academics. Similarly Annie, referring to how the National Student Survey may influence academics' responses to CPD, states that:

> I think it is a stick, rather than a carrot. I don't know, academics certainly in HE don't respond well to sticks. (Annie)

As has been shown, academics are working with changing national policy directives and increasing and shifting expectations are being made both on institutions and individuals (Cullingford 2002; D'Andrea and Gosling 2005). Potentially also, in response to some of these drivers, academics are experiencing change in organizational structures which impact upon practice. These changes, though, are arguably mitigated by continuity, for example, the spread of quality assurance practices may influence professional identity, but does not determine it (Knight 2002).

The CPD debates in practice: policy implementation

The relationship between national and institutional policy implementation, compounded by potential tensions related to the interface or 'duality' (Giddens 1981) between structure and agency, emerged as a further theme from the research. For example it was particularly notable that all interviewees – including key informants – agreed that there was no knowledge of an explicit, institution-wide concept, definition or philosophy with regard to CPD for its academics. For example, one key informant stated that 'there is a lot of very good practice that goes on, I just don't think it's agreed and standardized and embedded in processes, I think it is rooted in the culture.' Additionally when key informants were asked to identify where responsibility for CPD implementation was placed within the structure of the organization, it was apparent that the complexity of the concept is mirrored in the multifaceted nature of how it is supported in practice. Thus a range of central departments, along with the academic subject areas and the individual academics themselves, are all perceived as having some element of responsibility in this respect.

Earlier in this chapter the national context for CPD in academia was seen to have been set, at least in part, through the Higher Education Academy, by means of national professional standards and recognition through fellowship of the Academy. While the influence of these developments within the academic community is seen as 'a step in the right direction' (Annie), this research shows it to be severely limited. Of the 16 academics interviewed, four (25 per cent) were currently registered as Fellows of the HEA. While it should be acknowledged that some of the newer academics were working towards registration, many still perceived it as having little value or importance. When asked for views on the standards, Rhys said 'I don't know what the national standards are . . . can you give me a sort of rough idea?' Similarly Pascal, who had several years' teaching experience and a post-graduate certificate in education, was unaware that this may entitle him to apply for fellowship of the Academy.

It could be expected that the Academy's subject-centres network would have considerably influence on the practice and development needs of academics: this would follow from their propensity to focus professional development on discipline-related learning and the significance attributed to external networking with like-minded colleagues. However, this was found not to be the case. Few of those interviewed demonstrated any awareness of the subject centres, with those who were aware having little direct involvement:

> There is a subject centre for (my subject) and to be honest with you, I've never really heard anybody talk about it. (Chantrea)

> There is one, yes, but I think it's quite broad and our area is specific. (Catriona)

> I have looked at it, but not found it to be desperately useful which I was a bit disappointed with, I have to confess. (Peter)

The research therefore adds weight to the view that the connection between policy statement or intention on the one hand, and implementation through conception at institutional and individual level on the other, is at best uncertain and at worst nonexistent.

Conclusion

The tensions and debates raised through the literature, along with the additional and sometimes contrasting perspectives from academics analysed through this research, may have significant implications for academics' CPD in general and, more particularly, for the implementation of the *National Professional Standards for Teaching in Higher Education*. It can be seen that the notion of CPD is surrounded by a range of tensions and complexities that result in the concept being fluid, subjective and potentially attributed with a number of contestable meanings. Blackwell and Blackmore (2003b: 3) propose that not only is there 'no settled meaning', but that there is unlikely ever to be one. The participants in this research demonstrate that not only is there confusion over the meaning of CPD, but for many academics CPD as a concept is absent from their conscious thinking. As Clegg (2003b) suggests, there is an argument that problematizing the concept of CPD enables engagement in collegiate critique with regard to developing clarity of understanding; at the very least re-examining at individual and institutional levels how the term is conceptualized.

The voices of the academics in this research illustrate the rich and wideranging views on activities that enhance professional development. It is noticeable, however, that frequently academics do not perceive these activities as being developmental. Thus, the advancement of knowledge through social communication processes must not be jeopardized by institutional bureaucracy (Zuber-Skerritt 1992), as the quality of workplace environments can be seen as the central means of creating 'cultures of concern' and enhancing the quality of teaching and learning (Knight 2006). Indeed, the opportunity to develop CPD frameworks and policies that become accredited to the HEA can be seen as an opportunity to harness institutional, disciplinary and individual autonomy, as this facilitates the development of structures that recognize and value the whole range of academic professional development, being inclusive of all aspects of the academic role. Within this there needs to be clarity about whose needs are being met and who is responsible for CPD, with the connection between institutional processes and individual needs and aspirations being made explicit. In the following chapter Watling provides a useful example of developmental activity that raises the importance of acknowledging the diverse needs of all staff, as she discusses engagement with new technologies.

The research that has been reported through this chapter has considered how changes and continuities in contemporary higher education influence how academics perceive and respond to CPD. Through the perspective of academics themselves, a range of tensions and debates have been reinforced and illustrated. Perhaps Carla's pizza metaphor provides an apt conclusion here, in that there are many different 'recipes', many different 'flavours' being created in a complex and changing environment, so the pizzas that are CPD in higher education should rightly be subjected to analysis, debate and 'tasting' across academic cultures and institutional contexts.

Technology-Enhanced Learning: A New Digital Divide?

Sue Watling

7

Introduction

Changes in the way we communicate and access information are having a profound effect on the learning landscape. In the first decade of the twenty-first century, there is a growing need to 'adopt and adapt to the technological capabilities that allow information and communication to be distributed anywhere, anytime' (Anderson and Elloumi 2004: xiv). Virtual communication is evolving from a read-only environment to one that enables individual participation. No longer passive recipients of text, users can interact with content, contest meaning and construct new understandings. The internet is the host of a digital revolution and this evolution has identifiable phases; the first generation became known retrospectively as Web 1.0, we are currently experiencing Web 2.0 and there are already murmurings of a semantic Web 3.0 (Anderson 2007).

negative

The internet is an invasive medium which affects not only the educational sector but also the way we shop, bank and socialize, to name just a few of its incursions into daily life. Reliance on technology inevitably raises the question of equality of access. The term 'digital divide' was initially used to signify the difference between those with access to the technology and those without (Lenhart et al. 2002). While this remains a pertinent issue, the term as used in this chapter suggests there are other factors which need to be taken into account. The digital divide in higher education today is increasingly less about unequal access to computers and more about the unequal ways in which they are used (Warschauer et al. 2004).

Education developers in higher education are frequently asked: 'What is Web 2.0?' and the question itself may be seen as evidence of a growing new digital divide. The origins of the terms Web 1.0 and Web 2.0 may be contested but the differences between the two environments are clear. Underneath all the media hype, Web 2.0 applications frequently form the core of the online environment students are engaging with in the twenty-first century. Highly social and interactive, they are the antithesis of the VLEs embedded into contemporary university systems and practices. Web 2.0 applications such as Google and Wikipedia are prevalent in the student vocabulary, revealing their influence as students are faced with making relevant navigation choices through increasing quantities of information (JISC 2007, CIBER 2008). Social software provides peer support networks that often exist outside and beyond traditional campus provision. If technology is to be utilized effectively to enhance learning, educators need to keep up to date with student requirements, yet research into the student voice suggests that internet developments are outstripping institutional support at an alarming pace. The use of the World Wide Web is presenting a challenge; not only to long-established university structures but also to traditional models of teaching and learning (Laurillard 2002; Garrison and Anderson 2003).

By the end of the twentieth century the first wave of VLEs had been embedded into university infrastructures with an assurance they would transform the teaching experience. In the first decade of this new century, it appears they may have not only failed to live up to their early promise but actively contributed to growing evidence of a digital resistance. Prensky (2001) uses a pioneering analogy of 'digital natives' to describe those familiar with digital technologies compared with 'digital immigrants'; those adrift in an unfamiliar landscape of virtual communication. While division is rarely that simplistic, there is evidence that a gulf between the two, particularly in the educational sector, is widening. The skills of new generations of digital natives are increasingly embedded in Web 2.0 social tools and applications (CIBER 2008), leaving those who have yet to engage with online environments a challenging chasm to cross.

This chapter will examine the roots of this new multi-dimensional divide against the background of technology-enhanced learning in higher education. Looking first at the impact of online learning environments, it will uncover the tension between the conflicting demands of technology and the pedagogy and explore how this may have contributed towards resistance to digital delivery modes. As the read-only Web 1.0 environment transitioned into the collaborative, social world of Web 2.0, then a further strand can be added: the emerging identity of the digital student. Using the latest research into the voice of the student it will suggest answers to the question 'What is Web 2.0.' and assess implications for the university in the twenty-first century. The chapter will conclude with recommendations for policies and practices in order to build bridges across this new digital divide to enable internet technologies to become functionally embedded into existing systems and institutional strategies.

Technological challenges to traditional practices

It is in the nature of technology to challenge traditional practice. The Luddites of the eighteenth century are not only semantically similar to laggards resisting innovation today but they have a psychological affinity too. Within the higher education sector, resistance to technology-enhanced learning may be a key to a new digital divide, evidenced in particular in the gulf between the net savvy student and those still asking the question 'What is Web 2.0?' The current explosion of open source software, social networking and student preferences for Google and Wikipedia as research tools (JISC 2007; CIBER 2008), is widening the gap between those who engage with digital technology and those who still prefer the pen to the keyboard. Within higher education it is possible to identify the specific institutional origins of this resistance, which can be clearly traced to the initial introduction of technology-enhanced learning across the sector; it will be useful to examine these before looking at the nature and characteristics of the divide in more detail.

Universities are harbingers of convention, with a culture and historical identity that is supportive of 'academic tribes and practices' (Becher and Trowler 2001); they are traditionally resistant to change. The National Committee of Inquiry into Higher Education (NCIHE 1997) instigated a need to reassess practice and the report's recommendations included widening participation in higher education to a broader social base. Government targets were set at 50 per cent of 18–30 year olds having some experience of higher education by 2010. Further recommendations included harnessing the power of technology to provide the sector with the means to manage the quality and flexibility of its resources and delivery (NCIHE 1997; HEFCE 2005). Harnesses took the form of a new generation of educational technologies in the form of the Managed and the Virtual Learning Environments (MLE, VLE). These were presented as potential answers to the challenge of widening access and offering opportunities for broadening the sector's social base.

MLEs and VLEs were internet browser based systems containing information about all aspects of the student's learning experience in a digital format. The VLE was designed more specifically for supporting teaching and learning. Hosted by an institutional network, virtual environments were embedded into existing infrastructures with the promise of not only widening access but also transforming the teaching and learning experience. Initially, the focus rested on the technology. Attention was paid to systems integration and the processes of information management, rather than the implications for a change in practice (Laurillard 2002; Salmon 2005). Failure to recognize the complex and diverse requirements of teaching and learning was costly, as the majority of managerial policies neglected to acknowledge the need for research into pedagogical change. Institutions pasted new learning technology roles onto existing ones as institutional strategy often failed to recognize that traditional face-to-face teaching activities do not translate easily into an online environment (Garrison and Anderson 2003).

Significantly, the need to address this dual strand was not unforeseen. National strategy had clearly identified the need to ensure that research into the pedagogy of subject teaching was given full recognition and that support should be given at all stages to the development of the appropriate digital skills (HEFCE 2005). However, consultation at departmental level regarding the use of the new learning environment was frequently absent and innovators hampered by a lack of strategic guidance (Lisewski 2004). Top-down managerial approaches, resulting in pressure to participate, encouraged replication of existing transmission models. Rather than a catalyst for re-thinking pedagogical practice, VLEs were used primarily for hosting the presentational aspects of the traditional lecture.

The VLE was promoted as a one-size-fits-all model with an impressive brief. Promises were made for enhancement of the quality of teaching and learning, enabling accessibility and widening participation (HEFCE 2005) with little acknowledgement that all changes and innovations have inherent risk. Bell and Bell (2005) tell us that 70 per cent of innovations in education fail. Rather than being catalysts to transform the learning experience there was a tendency for VLEs to reinforce existing practice, particularly where there was reluctance to relinquish face-to-face methods of delivery (Salmon 2005). The VLE challenged not only conventional practice, but posed a threat to well established transmission models whereby the subject expert had control of the learning experience (Brown and Duguid 1995). Empowering the student and positioning the learner at the centre of their learning experience contested fundamental roles and practice. As Lamb (2004: 45) says: 'To truly empower students within collaborative or constructed activities requires the teacher to relinquish some degree of control over those activities.'

The well publicized demise of the UK e-university in 2004 appeared to support the belief that staff and students preferred contact with their colleagues rather than their computers (House of Commons 2005). Across the sector, there was a clear reluctance to abandon the lecture theatre and seminar room for a VLE without sound evidence for the benefits of doing so (Salmon 2005). Educators who recognized the need for a new pedagogical approach to learning technology advocated moving away from traditional modes of delivery and giving priority to constructivist models taking advantage of opportunities for online collaboration. Academic structures, such as the Five Step Model (Salmon 2000) and the Conversational Framework (Laurillard 2002), were instrumental in the transition of the learning process from a face-to-face environment into an online dialogue; a three way virtual inter-action between ideas, colleagues and tutors that supported the collaborative construction of knowledge. These cognitive processes endorsed the value of active engagement with content. Interaction was seen as the catalyst for creating both powerful learning experiences and constructing virtual 'communities of enquiry' for the stimulation of high levels of critical debate (Garrison and Anderson 2003).

The influence of the internet

There was no single point where the Web 1.0 technology underlying the VLE became known as Web 2.0. The transition was more a gradual development of existing platforms and applications (O'Reilly 2005; Anderson 2007). While there is no single definition of these terms, there are points of difference which clearly distinguish between them. Web 1.0 enabled users with the appropriate skills to publish text and images online. The need for a specific skill set helped ensure controls remained in the hands of the few; the implications of this for higher education being an emphasis on 'how' the technology worked rather than 'why' it should be utilized. The learning curve for the non-technical individual was high. With few positive examples to demonstrate enhancement of learning, the barrier of technological competence remained unchallenged. Online resources were not hugely exciting. File compression was in its infancy, and narrow bandwidths limited the use of multimedia. As a result, the Web 1.0 phase of internet, and the VLE it supported, consisted mainly of text and still images. In the majority of cases, audio and video provision was patchy and problematic, and opportunities for interaction were virtually non-existent.

Web 2.0 tackled the issue of user involvement head on. It provided a different environment, one which offered file compression supporting the production of digital audio (mp3 podcasts) and digital video (mp4 videocasts). This in turn stimulated the production of reusable online learning objects. National repositories of resources such as Jorum (UK) and Merlot (US) offered free access to a broad mix of educational and often interactive blocks of learning. Dramatic shrinkage in download times eased resource transmission. The capacity of data storage devices increased while they became increasingly portable. The Web 2.0 environment matured alongside technology that was wireless and mobile. Laptops could connect to the internet without network sockets and cables. GPS enabled mobile phones offered an 'anytime, anywhere' online experience. Whereas Web 1.0 was static, Web 2.0 is dynamic, with an architecture based on open source software, one which frees the user from the restraints of commercially available programs and ensures applications are freely available to download. Interaction through social software such as blogs, wikis and bookmarking has constructed a new and vibrant network of communication systems with interaction between content and users at the centre. The resulting interactive network of communications closely resembled the original vision for the World Wide Web, which envisaged the putting in of ideas as well as taking them out.

> I wanted the Web to be what I call an interactive space where everyone can edit. And I started saying 'interactive', and then I read in the media that the Web was great because it was 'interactive', meaning you could click. This was not what I meant by interactivity. (Berners-Lee 1997)

This interaction and the transfer and exchange of information supported a founding principle of the Web 2.0 environment: the more it is used the more it improves (O'Reilly 2005). As creators, sharers and editors of information, the participants themselves have value, not just as consumers but as innovators and agents of change. The user of Web 2.0 is also the creator of Web 2.0. Syndication threads track information changes and inform users of new content; tags enable the creation of categories, organizing and sharing information systems relevant to individual requirements. Web 2.0 technologies ensure the individual has a voice that can be heard and responded to with a significant amount of user control over virtual worlds and experiences.

If the pedagogical challenge of the VLE was radical, then the challenges of Web 2.0 are even greater, especially for those at the pen end of the digital divide. There is a new vocabulary to be mastered, for example blog, wiki, tag clouds and mashups. Software has deliberately mis-spelt names like Flickr, Digg and Scribblar. Emphasis on the social benefits of the programs ensures users can freely personalize their own virtual environment and take advantage of a flexibility which offers multiple choices about where, when and how to interact online. Once Massively Multiplayer Online games (MMOs), and active immersive 3D virtual worlds such as Second Life are added into the mix of technologies available for educational innovation, then a threshold point is created along the continuum of online learning engagement; one which becomes indicative of the new digital divide.

Virtual Learning Environments have not been entirely left behind. The majority of institutions still support some form of browser based platform; either open source software such as Moodle or a managed environment system like Blackboard, and in recognition of the new collaborative opportunities of the internet, VLEs now incorporate additional plug-in tools.

Blogs and wikis

Opportunities for collaboration via collaborative tools such as blogs (or Web-logs) and wikis, both synonymous with the term Web 2.0, are becoming more frequent and both are increasingly being evaluated for their educational potential. Blogs and wikis consist of online web pages with a text editor facility. This enables users to have an internet presence with a minimum of technical knowledge. They are markedly different environments compared to the first generation websites and VLEs. Their open nature ensures they can be publicly available, unlike an institutional network which is restricted to registered users and hidden behind user identification names and passwords. Crucially, neither the blog nor the wiki were designed exclusively for educational purposes and this independent existence may be one of their greatest strengths. The VLE was developed to support learning. As a result there was a tendency for the technology behind it to drive the policies designed to ensure engagement. Web 2.0 tools such as blogs and wikis have no allegiance to the educational sector and exist independently from corporate control. This ensures they can be adapted and used to support learning in response to individual requirements; processes evident from their early use within the educational sector.

The blog has been the core of personal internet publishing. Popular for its cross-discipline nature and capacity for objective public debate, its challenge to traditional academic behaviour was part of the early attraction. As Farrell (2005), a founding member of the first academic blog *Crooked Timbers* says '[blogs] are likely to transform how we think of ourselves as scholars. While blogging won't replace academic publishing, it builds a space for serious conversation around and between the more considered articles and monographs that we write'.

Unlike formal participation on a VLE discussion board, blogging traditionally incorporates a personal point of view. Blogs have been adopted as tools for reflection; their value extended by the opportunity for readers to post comments on blog entries. In addition, the software is designed to encourage users to personalize their individual online space. It has been suggested that the ability to personalize, and the subsequent sense of ownership, is conducive to wider participation. Also, the social nature of blogs, with their freedom from institutional controls, can actively encourage a broader range of perspectives (Downes 2004). Unlike the blog where comments are read-only, the wiki combines reading with the facility to edit, enabling online communities to interact and collaborate on shared documents. Wikipedia, the online encyclopaedia based on wiki technology, is increasingly popular with students (CIBER 2008). Perceived as lacking academic credibility, it was famously challenged against the Encyclopaedia Britannica. A similar number of mistakes were discovered in each; the wiki having the advantage that its errors could be corrected in seconds (Giles 2005). The wiki is an embodiment of Open Source software with a structure shaped and defined by its users. Functioning on the ethic of 'SoftSecurity' it is reliant on the community to enforce order, a treatise which has proved dependable within the Web 2.0 platform. As Lamb (2004: 40) says 'The proportion of fixers to breakers tends to be high, and a wiki will generally have little difficulty remaining stable'.

The effect of increasingly digital lifestyles on education providers

Developments and advances in mobile and wireless access ensure that exposure to the internet is continually widening. The prevalence of digital technology means that a new generation has grown up in a predominantly electronic environment. Research suggests that increasing exposure to digitization is creating new brain patterns which may have a significant impact for teaching the learners of the future. Prensky (2001) claims that these digital lifestyles have created a new generation of digital natives who are comfortable with virtual communication. Those who find themselves adrift in this new world are the digital immigrants, speaking 'an outdated language (that of the pre-digital age) [and they] are struggling to teach a population that speaks an entirely new language' Prensky (2001: 2). Research within the United States suggests that digital competency is leading to significant shifts in lifestyle (Oblinger and Oblinger 2005). Findings include a tendency for students who can select from a previously unimaginable quantity of digital information to become more strategic, only expressing interest in what they feel they need to know. Levels of concentration appear increasingly short-lived. Instant communication via text or instant messaging is favoured and the ability to multi-task is commonly reported. The majority of students exhibit a 'bricolage' behaviour pattern where their preferred style of learning is discovery-based; exploring and manipulating a multiplicity of media (Hartman et al. 2005).

Research across the educational sector in the United Kingdom also reveals a range of new competencies and preferences, suggesting that digital learners of the future are unlikely to have a single voice (Rudd et al. 2006). Research within higher education strongly suggests that technical skills are not synonymous with the ability to learn online, reflecting the divide between the technology and pedagogy (Sharpe and Benfield 2005). In 2006, the Joint Information Systems Committee (JISC) carried out two studies; LEX, the JISC Learner Experience of eLearning (Creanor et al. 2006) and LXP, the JISC Student Experiences of Technologies (Conole et al. 2006). The findings show a wide dependence on the internet and mobile technology (JISC 2007). They provide the strongest evidence yet for a widening divide between those who use the internet as part of their daily life, and are comfortable with the digital enhancement of learning, and those at the opposite end of the continuum who have yet to begin their engagement.

The key findings from the learner's voice (Creanor et al. 2006) demonstrate clear evidence that students' lifestyles are increasingly digital. There is frequent reference to strong peer support networks via email, texting and online messaging which suggest high levels of social interaction between students. Digital networking provides a personal support system both on and off campus with personal mobile phones, laptops and PDAs all cited as playing a constituent role in their learning experiences. This is not always mirrored by staff. 'I think it depends on the teacher really . . . if they're on board with it a hundred and ten percent then you'll be included. If they're not then they won't use it and neither will you' (Creanor et al. 2006: 16). Both reports reveal reluctance by academic staff to be involved with learning online: 'the tutor was, like, "I've never seen this [online resource] before and I don't even know what it is and I hope I don't have to get involved in it"' (JISC 2007: 23). The university of the twenty-first century needs the prerequisite skills to understand the challenges of a digital lifestyle and there are a growing number of educators suggesting that 'claims of technical illiteracy' have no viable future (Fisch 2007). The prevalence of the internet as revealed in the voice of the learners suggests a growing need for teaching and support staff to be equipped to deal with digital competencies and lifestyles.

The reports also clearly indicate how student familiarity with a range of personal technologies, and the opportunities to personalize their learning environment, gives them confidence with a range of digital tools, for example a mobile phone can offer multiple methods of communication:

> I use my phone because it's like a mobile internet to me . . . unlike the email [where] I need to go on the computer and open my mail box; but with the mobile phone, I can get any communication any time I want. (JISC 2007: 21)

Great importance is attached to digital tools, and students are reluctant to give them up even if this causes conflict with technical support once they arrive at university. 'I use my laptop. I take it away, it's attached to me, I couldn't survive without it' (JISC 2007: 18). There is a clear implication here for institutional policy. As well as supporting a corporate network, an additional infrastructure for testing the effectiveness and appropriateness of new technologies and applications would extend student technological support to a wider range of open source options; ones which it is increasingly likely students will be expecting to find and use.

There is also evidence that student confidence with technology may be superficial. A lack of depth is particularly clear when searching for information online. Digital students demonstrate a tendency to take findings at face value and spend insufficient time evaluating accuracy or relevance. The skills required to make appropriate choices are frequently absent. Internet search engines, in particular, Google, and collaborative websites such as Wikipedia are preferred to libraries and learning centre provision for information retrieval:

> Well, I use Google almost every day. And it actually turns up quite a bit of scientific data and if you go to 'Limit', or do a special search or detailed search, you can limit things down too. Well, you can take off .dot or .co.uk sites and then it tends to give you back scientific sites and I turn up quite a bit of information through that. (JISC 2007: 19)

Students cite the low cost compared to purchasing text books and the convenience of going online compared to travelling. 'They're [tutors] saying use books but books cost money so the internet is the main thing that we end up using' (JISC 2007: 23). These findings are reinforced by research commissioned by the British Library and JISC to identify the information behaviour of the researcher of the future (CIBER 2008). An over reliance on Google Scholar, a lack of effective research strategies and 'power browsing' through titles, content pages and abstracts are all cited by CIBER as evidence that electronic publishing and mass digitization are making it increasingly difficult for students to focus on text in depth. 'Everyone exhibits a bouncing/flicking behaviour, which sees them searching horizontally rather than vertically. Power browsing and viewing is the norm for all' (CIBER 2008: 8). As the internet opens up new possibilities for research, institutions may have to accept they can no longer remain in total control of access to information and that strategies need to ensure an increased focus on technical support and information literacy skills. The research shows that IT confidence should not be mistaken for IT competence and that digital literacy skills are essential for effective use of search engines and assessing the accuracy and relevance of online content.

Emerging good practice

Research into the use of digital technology to enhance the teaching and learning experience is currently funded by a number of national organizations. These provide strategic information to enable institutional policy-makers to make informed decisions that are relevant to their own e-learning initiatives.

The Joint Information Systems Committee (JISC), already mentioned in this chapter for their research into the student experience of online learning and digital resources, provides funding for a wide range of research into the innovative use of ICT across the further and higher education sectors (Anderson 2007; JISC 2007). Their strategic themes include e-learning, e-research and e-resources. JISC-supported services include JISC InfoNet which offers advice on the management of ICT to support teaching and research, and Intute which provides free access to examples of educational web resources.

JISC is an implementation partner of the HEFCE e-learning strategy (HEFCE 2005) along with the Higher Education Academy (HEA). The HEA works to enhance the higher education teaching and learning experience and, with JISC, has led the Pathfinder Project which included an e-learning benchmarking exercise to analyse institutional e-learning provision and processes, and funding for e-learning Pathfinder Projects designed to implement organizational change (Morrison 2008).

The Beyond Distance Research Alliance at The University of Leicester manages a number of Pathfinder Projects including the Advanced Design for E-Learning: Institutional Embedding (AMELIE) and the Informal Mobile Podcasting and Learning Adaptation (IMPALA). It has also created the virtual Media Zoo; an experimental online area for staff researching into the educational use of digital technologies.

The HEA funds 24 Regional Subject Centres who are all taking part in the HEA Distributed e-Learning programme (DeL) looking to engage with the HEFCE e-learning strategy and research into the use of technologies to support learning and teaching. HEA also works in strategic partnership with the Heads of e-Learning Forum (HeLF), relevant Centres for Excellence in Teaching and Learning (CETLs) and the Association for Learning Technology (ALT); all with a remit to research into the use of digital technologies to enhance the teaching and learning experience.

The Observatory on Borderless Higher Education (OBHE) is an international strategic information service and one of the leading sources of strategic information on transnational higher education. 170 organizational subscribers represent 50 countries worldwide; all being engaged in various aspects of transnational higher education and dedicated to sharing of their institutional experiences relating to the planning and managing of e-learning.

At the University of Lincoln, the Centre for Educational Research and Development (CERD) has tackled the issue of the digital divide by setting up an online LearningLab; an experimental area for staff which is dedicated to investigating how Web 2.0 tools can further enhance teaching and learning. Current research in CERD includes an extensive study of the student experience of online learning (Watling unpublished) and the use of templates to create customizable online learning objects.

Conclusion

It may not be possible to predict the future of higher education but it will almost certainly be increasingly digital. This chapter has tried to show how developments in virtual technologies have resulted in a continuum of engagement among academic staff with a threshold point dividing those who are familiar with the new digital tools and those who still prefer a pen to a keyboard. The implications of this divide for those at the pen end of the continuum are significant. Many students arrive on campus with increasingly digital lifestyles; accustomed to access to multiple virtual landscapes. If the university of the twenty-first century is to be equipped to deal with the digital student, it must have systems and staff who are prepared to be digital too.

The internet has been called a 'disruptive technology' because it is a powerful agent for change (Anderson and Elloumi 2004). Its evolving systems of information management and social software present challenges to institutional policy which must effectively embed new technologies into existing systems and also be responsible for the diverse needs of staff engaging with them. As Beckton says in Chapter 5, there is an argument for a subtle response to enhancement but, according to Crawford (Chapter 6), the responsibility for ensuring staff continuing and professional development is far from being clearly delineated. This chapter shows how information literacy must become a fundamental part of the teaching toolbox and corporate networks have to acknowledge the need to be responsive to a diverse range of digital environments.

How can this be done? The internet and the educational sector share common foundations of knowledge and communication. It should be possible for them to augment each other rather than be divisive and for structures to be identified for creating links between the two. These bridges may include ensuring that future policies work towards a more holistic approach, creating flexible systems which can respond to new internet developments. Traditional transmission models could be translated into collaborative online activities and staff offered the apposite training and support for appropriate use of these new online environments. There is no single mechanism which would narrow the digital divide, and no single path across it; even if there were, it might not be the most effective option. Instead, the concept of building bridges to support both the technology and the pedagogy, allowing two-way traffic between both the analogue and the digital experiences of staff and students, would provide the opportunity to meet in the middle at whichever point is most appropriate for individual needs and lifestyles.

Part Three
The Student Experience

Part Three explores the ways in which universities are capable of being transformed through progressive forms of engagement with their students. Each of the chapters deals with a different dimension of student engagement: student intelligence, the stretched academy and the student as producer.

Hagyard deals with the student engagement through the notion of student intelligence, by which he means the ways in which surveying student opinion has become an important activity for universities. This discussion is contextualized with reference to the National Student Survey launched in 2005, and the way in which it has been implemented at the University of Lincoln. Hagyard challenges two aspects of conventional wisdom concerning online surveys: the impossibility of high response rates and the argument that students suffer from survey fatigue. High response rates, he argues, are achievable with appropriate online tools chosen for ease of use, including personalized emails and automatic reminders to non-respondents. Survey fatigue can be minimized if surveys are presented as part of a well-managed feedback system. Hagyard argues that surveys provide external accountability and ways in which universities can benchmark themselves against other higher education institutions. They also give access to detailed data to which universities can respond in order to enhance the student experience. His recommendations are systemic and cultural: he argues that student feedback should be collected in robust and rigorous ways as part of continuous process of quality enhancement.

Morris extends this focus on the student experience by looking at students from the lowest socio-economic groups who, she argues, are in danger of being discriminated against by the stretched academy. For Morris, the stretched academy is characterized by limited resources and heavy staff workloads, leading to content-driven teaching styles and an aversion to experiential teaching methods. While the stretched academy has indeed widened participation, there are still only low numbers of students from the lowest socio-economic groups; their participation has done nothing to challenge the academy's elitist pretensions. The real issue is how universities can be changed – or stretched in a different way – so they are more inclusive and encourage participation and achievement in the fullest sense, creating a new form of democratic learning between lecturers and students.

Neary and Winn argue that the success of the modern university is in danger of being undermined by too close an attachment to the imperatives of market economics. They argue that one outcome of this process of commercialization is to transform the student into a consumer, overly preoccupied with employability, under-employment, poverty and debt. They suggest that an alternative approach to student consumerism is the idea of the student as producer, a collaborative relationship between student and teacher resulting in the production of work of academic content and value.

They also argue that the current preoccupation with the commercialization of knowledge as intellectual property operates as a form of restriction on the generalizability of scientific knowledge, which is crucial to the scientific enterprise. They identify forms of knowledge collection and dissemination based on progressive legal devices and new digital technologies which, they argue, will result in the undermining of the dominant discourse of knowledge privatization by means of intellectual property pedagogy within the universities themselves and lead to students taking a more proactive role in the production of knowledge.

The Stretched Academy: The Learning Experience of Mature Students from Under-represented Groups

8

Aileen Morris

Introduction

As Stevenson and Bell argued in Chapter 1, government and Higher Education Funding Council for England (HEFCE) policy on widening participation has stated that 'education must be a force for opportunity and social justice, not the entrenchment of privilege' (HEFCE 2002a). In the past 30 years, higher education has been stretched to become a mass education system partly through an increase in the numbers of school leavers attending universities and partly through an expansion of the numbers of mature students and those from social groups that are not widely represented in higher education (Scott 1995). The tensions produced by this government-led imperative to increase numbers entering higher education while, at the same time, reducing the overall unit of resource available, have led to some significant changes in many of our higher education institutions, the outcomes of which have sometimes been referred to as 'stretching the academy' (Thompson, 2000).

Partly as a result of these changes the student learner and the learning experience have been the focus for much research and debate. Training programmes for staff in the post-compulsory sector have been marked by the emphasis on the individual. The most significant of these programmes, the PGCE (Post-Graduate Certificate in Education), focuses on skills and knowledge around learning and teaching, the usefulness of reflective practice and the primacy of the individual learner. The curriculum offered does indeed cover 'barriers to learning', but can tend to view these as emanating from the individual student, to be countered either through the actions of the student and tutor working together or, significantly, by the intervention of other support agencies. Barriers emanating from the institution are acknowledged, but tend to be seen as deep-rooted and unchangeable; the emphasis is on mitigating the effects of these. Recent changes in higher education have made the mature student's learning experience increasingly difficult, particularly for those students who continue to be under-represented in our universities: those defined as working class, disabled, or from ethnic minority groups. What is explored here is the prediction that, as a result of growth in the higher education sector, 'the student's experience will be more isolated but less insulated' (Haselgrove 1994: 172). One of the questions to be asked is if we – who teach and support in the higher education sector – are, in some ways, propping up a system that by its nature discriminates against and seeks to normalize those mature students from lower socio-economic groups (Bowl 2003).

Initially, this chapter will develop the arguments outlined in Chapter 1 by looking at some of the main initiatives and resulting changes currently being worked through in higher education as a result of government policy and pedagogical thinking. There follows an account of these changes on the learning experiences of mature higher education students from under-represented groups, specifically those drawn from the lower socio-economic groupings, and an exploration of how the changes diminish and reduce those students' experiences. Finally, the chapter will draw together some ideas around how change needs to take place at a more fundamental level if participation in the higher education learning experience, in the fullest sense, is to be achieved.

Stretching the academy: participation and resources

According to Thompson, the widening participation initiative is one sense in which the academy has been stretched. This is 'largely as a response to the economic implications of globalisation, but also in the interests of social inclusion' (Thompson 2000: 2). Increases in the number of students from lower socio-economic groups have been uneven across the higher education sector. Although an increase has taken place in the traditional universities, much of the stretching has been done by the newer higher education institutions and those that have been used to change (Watson and Taylor 1998: 39). Nevertheless, higher education, once the preserve of an elite group, has become more widely available to people from lower socio-economic groups.

What is important, however, is that this widening, or increase, as some have described it, still only includes a small minority of those from the lowest socio-economic groupings. Furthermore this expansion has been matched, in some senses, by a more clearly stratified and fragmented higher education system where 'new forms of inequality' have emerged via government rhetoric around 'choice' (Reay et al. 2005). Nonetheless, mature students (those over 21) have accounted for much of the expansion in student numbers. Indeed, this growth has been three times as rapid for mature students generally as for young people, and most rapid among mature women. The discussion here will focus on those who are described as first generation entrants, both men and women, and who are, additionally, drawn from those socio-economic groups that are under-represented in higher education.

The academy has also been stretched in another sense. Changes in how universities are funded in the last two decades have led to financial difficulties in many of those institutions that have responded to the 'economic and non-economic drivers' of higher education (Thomas 2001: 5). The results of this under-funding have been various but have generally led to a trend in higher education that is concerned with 'greater efficiency through reducing teaching costs per student' (Bamber et al. 2000). Coupled with an institutional emphasis on 'New Labour's version of . . . the perceived centrality of the learner, and the accompanying rhetoric of self-directed learning, the contemporary policy context' (Taylor 2000: 68), this has, paradoxically, resulted in there being fewer – and different – learning and teaching resources available for mature students coming into higher education from under-represented socio-economic groups. This was predicted by McGivney:

> The steady cuts in universities' finance and staffing over the last decade, together with proposed cuts in the numbers of lecturers . . . suggest a service that is shrinking at the same time that it is required to expand. (McGivney 1990: 181)

In the stretched academy, change has taken place in many ways. Although these changes have influenced the learning experience of the whole student body, the learning landscape of mature students has been uniquely affected.

The stretched academy: consequences for the student experience

It is recognized that the changes described will not be experienced in the same way by all mature students from lower socio-economic groups.

Read et al. (2003) note that individuals do not merely passively receive discourses of academic culture. They actively engage with those discourses and sometimes challenge them. Nonetheless, such students are now encountering an altered set of resources to meet their needs. This is not to say that previous provision within the higher education sector was one that welcomed non-traditional students and made their learning experience a relevant and meaningful encounter. It is to say that increased demands upon existing resources have led to a more instrumental approach to the education that is on offer to all students in higher education: 'buying learning is no different from buying a car, or a packet of cornflakes' (Taylor 2000: 76). Higher education has become a business with consumers (students), costs (staff, rooms, resources) and targets (retention, achievement, progression). In the new stretched academy, students are viewed as customers or clients, knowledge is a commodity to be bought, and success is measured in terms of targets (Thompson 2000).

Traditionally, the university was considered a place apart: where, as Karran notes in Chapter 2, those fortunate enough to enter its portals would be able to embrace new ideas, think critically and reflect upon all manner of things. In other words, the university was a place whose 'project is to emancipate its students through a process of critical self reflection' (Scott 1995: 4). Although there has been some criticism of this liberal tradition in education (Taylor 2000: 72–3), the idea of emancipation for the learner and the concept of education as having a wider social purpose are still regarded as very attractive, both inside and outside higher education. The new emphasis is on learners as individuals who should have control over what, when and how they study. This is appealing because it seems to be about how the system can respond to the student's needs. Taylor (2000) explores the idea of the self-directed learner within higher education and the New Labour repackaging of it. He also argues that this concept of learning is based on what is an essentially individualistic perspective. This is articulated in the policies and initiatives of the late 1990s in HEFCE's *Widening Participation* documents (Taylor 2000).

This view of the learner as both individual and self-directed, and as a consumer of education has clear implications for the mature student from under-represented groups in terms of power. A strong critique of this is that the idea of the independent learner is 'based on an ethnocentric masculinist ideal of a "traditional" student unencumbered by domestic responsibilities, poverty or the need for support' (Leathwood 2001, in Read et al. 2003). This view of the student may well seem an attractive proposition for the stretched and under-resourced academy. Read et al. (2003) also found that some students have 'constructed a

self-identity as "consumer" that enables them to hold a position of great
but, given the rhetoric of choice and the marketization of higher educat

> Should those who pay more, or shout louder, receive a 'better' service? Should
> those who are exempt from paying fees [or receive institutional bursaries] have
> fewer 'rights' as a consumer than those who are entirely self-funded? (Read et al.
> 2003: 274)

The sort of provision being offered and the nature of the student's learning experience are also called in question, since the consumerist perspective in higher education ultimately reduces the perceived benefits of learning – at this level and in this context – to employability and market returns. 'The role of the radical educator is to encourage and support the democratic and progressive articulation of self-directed learning and to oppose the more reactionary and negative perspectives' (Taylor 2000: 77).

Ideologically, the centrality of the learner stems from a humanistic approach to learning and teaching (Rogers 1983). Building on these ideas, Knowles (1984) developed his theories of andragogy. This approach sees the learner as active, and the process of learning being one that includes the personal involvement of the learner: discovery, reflection, working with others and developing skills in critical thinking and evaluation. It sees learners as being able to a large extent to control their learning, with tutors as facilitators. Many of the skills required by the practitioner as facilitator are those that draw on traditional counselling skills: listening, responding, questioning and summarizing. Although it is not advocated here that we import Knowles' ideas wholesale into our pedagogic practice, these approaches to learning and teaching have been recognized as having value for all students and not just those that are being discussed here. Opportunities for learning as described above, where the student is seen to play a central role and is involved in more dynamic and active ways, have become constricted in the stretched academy because contact with tutors is reduced and there is still a great reliance on teacher-focused approaches to learning. This can be seen by some tutors as labour-intensive and time-consuming; sometimes, unnecessarily so. Indeed, the introduction of new groups of students and innovatory practices has been perceived in some institutions to be a threat both to staff roles (McGivney 1990) and, some may say, to the purpose of a university. The view persists in some quarters that 'adults [should] suspend their adulthood at the door of the institution . . . by their situational acceptance of the authority of the tutor' and that experience can be a 'block to learning' (Hanson 1996, quoted in Peters et al. 1999).

McGivney believed that there were many misconceptions about adult learners and saw a need for extensive staff development programmes. Interestingly, this is echoed by students in their feedback for the recent Higher Education Policy Institute (HEPI) study (Sastry and Bekhradnia 2007) where students identified better training for lecturers as being third most important out of fourteen priorities for further investment. Traditional teaching methods and styles coupled with the inability, or reluctance, to revise and develop learning and teaching practice can only have a detrimental effect on mature students from under-represented socio-economic groups.

Higher education continues to be dominated by traditional teaching methods: lectures, seminars and tutorials. Lectures continue in the traditional format with large numbers of students in lecture theatres (Lammers and Murphy 2002). In terms of student learning lectures do serve a purpose, albeit limited (Bligh 1972; McLeish 1976, in Biggs 2003: 100) in that they can be 'ineffective in stimulating higher-order thinking' and can encourage a surface approach to learning as opposed to deep-learning (Marton and Säljö 1997). Lectures also assume that the student feels reasonably confident in this situation and knows what to do in order to take some useful learning away with them.

It is generally accepted that the seminar should be an attempt to engage the students in more interactive group activities, an opportunity for issues and ideas from lectures to be explored further in the context of the lived experience. It is where the student can be 'helped to move to a more abstract, theoretical, contextualising investigation of reality' (Murphy and Fleming 1998: 5). In the stretched academy, however, seminars where content-dominated learning outcomes often predominate can be little more than mini-lectures with some opportunity for question and answer. One of the reasons for this is that the number of students in seminar groups has increased. It is important to add that the seminar group can often consist of considerably more than the 15 used in the recent study by Sastry and Bekhradnia (2007) for HEPI; this can work against some of the opportunities for close and interactive work that seminars can offer. Both experienced and less experienced staff will tend to use more traditional transmission methods of teaching rather than risk trying to manage a whole group discussion or small group work when they do not know students' names, feel pressured to cover content and meet the demands of assessment protocols.

Tutorials have traditionally been very valuable for students as opportunities for one-to-one contact with the tutor and occasions when detailed feedback and discussion can take place on a variety of learning matters. In the stretched academy, opportunities for such tutorials have become rarer. Tutorials tend to be used as occasions when students can negotiate a topic for a piece of work or be monitored in terms of their progress. They tend not to be used as times when a student can discuss an issue of interest arising out of the learning or even receive verbal feedback on assessed work. In the time-pressed curriculum, there is often little negotiation about dates and times of tutorials; this can pose a problem for mature students who have considerable domestic responsibilities, feel less confident in interactions with the tutors and less worthy of the tutor's time. The recent development of tutorial contact via email has become more common; for some it has to some degree replaced face-to-face tutorials and this has implications for students who value more traditional forms of contact: 'For many post 1992 universities, the *personal* [my italics] contact of small-group tuition could mean the difference between a student from a widening participation background reaching graduation day or dropping out' (Fearn 2008).

Given the changes outlined, it is clear that quality contact with the tutor and opportunities for discussion and debate in the stretched academy have become rarer. Even the need to enter the university buildings diminishes with comparatively low contact hours, reduced opportunities for learning in small teaching groups (Sastry and Bekhradnia 2007), and the fact that learning materials, lecture notes and details of assessments can be downloaded from the university's VLE. Malcolm (2000) argues that the relationship between students, peers and their teachers has been transformed. She goes on to add (remembering her own higher education experience): 'The secure leisured aimlessness and pedagogic inertia of the useless lecturers of yesteryear will have been replaced by something else, but it will not necessarily be any better' (Malcolm 2000: 19). To what extent have these transformations in the learning landscape affected the higher education experience of mature students from under-represented socio-economic groups?

The learning landscape of mature students

When mature students from the under-represented socio-economic groups enter higher education, they are entering an alien environment

(Read et al. 2003). As Scott (1995: 2) asserts, higher education 'has become a mass system in its public structures but remains an elite one in its private instincts'. This is echoed in Gorard et al.'s report to HEFCE (2006) when they observe that higher education was not intended to be available to all and is, unlike other lifelong educational opportunities, based on selective entry. Historically, the university system existed to educate the elite and prepare them for their roles as decision and policy makers at the highest levels in society. This view of the purpose of higher education remains today although it is now the choice and location of the university or college, and the level and nature of programmes that will distinguish the elite from others within the system (Reay et al. 2007). Higher education, as it is constructed, is to some degree beyond the student's 'habitus' in that it is outside their past, present and continuing experience. As the first family member to enter higher education, the mature student from under-represented socio-economic groups is entering not only an unknown environment but, at times, a hostile one. The university 'is not a neutral environment; it is value laden' (Thomas 2001: 121).

Tett asked a sample of non-traditional students who they thought higher education was for. Their responses 'showed their awareness of the structural inequalities that impeded their transition to becoming university students, rather than seeing their non-participation as solely the result of a personal lack of ability' (Tett 2000:188). As Bamber et al. comment: 'class is real and operative, not abstract . . . making higher education hard to survive' (Bamber et al. 2000: 169). Similarly, in research into young working class participants' accounts of learning in Scottish institutions a set of differentiated experiences of higher education were reported and one commented:

> I didn't feel working class until I went to uni, because I'm not particularly working class. But now I feel *incredibly* working class and I feel like a wee socialist that stands up for what she believes in. (Forsyth and Furlong 2000: 36–7)

Even for those mature students who have completed an Access programme prior to their university degree course it is not surprising that, given their new and alien environment, confidence is a key problem for many mature students from under- represented groups, particularly in their first year. Personal contact with approachable tutors where information can be shared and feedback given is very important in helping the student to feel more at ease. Ryan reported research which looked at the barriers to success in higher education experienced by one mature woman returner, Betty, both pre-entry and during the programme. In terms of support for her learning and feed-back on her progress, Betty remembers:

> It's not that they didn't give you confidence, it was the reassurance they didn't give me – they all said 'we haven't got a problem with you.' (Ryan 2001: 3)

Ryan comments:

> The feeling of not being supported was compounded by the lack of access and time with tutors who, according to Betty, were all studying for their own MSc's and had their own agendas. (Ryan 2001: 3)

Holland argues that Access and Widening Participation strategies succeed or fail at the level of each academic department and discipline. She notes that 'confidence remains the biggest issue inhibiting students from a sense that they can participate fully in the processes of questioning and risk-taking that a degree . . . will demand of them' and also that 'it is important for [lec-turers] to establish environments which foster student confidence' (Holland 2003: 15). She also observes that lecturers need to value the different kinds of experience that students actually have rather than the cultural knowledge they may be assumed to possess.

Prosser and Trigwell point out that students entering higher education form particular perceptions of their situation. The tutor will have set up the learning situation with specific approaches and tasks in mind. Learners will 'not necessarily perceive their situation in the way it was designed' (Prosser and Trigwell 1999: 64). Different learners will perceive the learning situation differently. This variation, they go on to say:

> [R]esults from the interaction between the students' prior experiences of similar learning and teaching situations and the particular context within which they are placed. Those perceptions, in turn, are related to the way the students approach their learning in that context. (Prosser and Trigwell 1999: 64)

If these perceptions are, in part, based on relational experiences of learn-ing then, for mature students from under-represented groups, there may well be an absence of 'similar learning and teaching situations' or a learning experience which speaks of failure and has negative connotations. Prosser and Trigwell argue that when considering the quality of the learning experience for students, the task for university tutors should not be 'trying to change the student, but . . . trying to change the context experienced by the student' (Prosser and Trigwell 1999: 7). In the stretched academy, this context is already undergoing change. The issue here is whether this change is going to be such that it will offer the mature student from under-represented groups a learning experience that takes account of, and values, their perceptions and experience.

Mature students who have completed an Access to Higher Education programme before coming to university often cite their fellow students as providing essential mutual support during their studies. Often there will have been opportunities while on the Access programme – usually at the beginning – to share their histories, anxieties, hopes and fears. Given the large numbers of students in the stretched academy and the traditional approaches to teaching and learning (encouraged by the system in terms of the design and use of teaching and learning spaces), these experiential and student-centred approaches are, effectively, discouraged. In the study by Ryan (2001) mentioned earlier, she reports on the difficulties Betty faced when she joined her degree course:

> It was not very clear at all what they wanted . . . you were just paddling around in a big sea really and it was because we were all paddling around together that we held each other up. (Ryan 2001: 2)

Modularization of the curriculum has also had its effect upon the mature student's learning experience, as they are less likely to form the tightly-knit peer support groups that students have recounted as being invaluable for their survival in the higher education system. As they move between their unit options and peer learning groups over the course of three years, students' experience becomes more fragmented and networks of support are harder to form and maintain. Scott (1995) states that given modularized programmes, students need support in constructing a coherent curriculum for themselves early in their higher education learning experience. Furthermore, the fragmented nature of programmes will inhibit the opportunities for connected and creative thinking that higher education can offer. Although pedagogic emphasis is placed on the student as an individual learner, it is argued here that any control over learning and its processes has, in reality, shifted away from the learner. The learning experience has moved to one where students remain generally passive and, to some extent, isolated from both their peers and their tutors.

Re-empowering the mature learner

The focus upon the individual student and achievement represents in some ways a welcome shift but in others a serious flaw, given that the focus upon the individual will 'exclude consideration of the collective, the group needs' (Taylor 2000: 76). Mature students from under-represented groups draw confidence and, ultimately, strength from each other when studying, whether on an Access programme in further education or on a degree programme in higher education. Those from similar social backgrounds confronting the alienation of higher education for the first time can, where the opportunity arises, tend to come together fairly early on in their studies. This is echoed by Betty above in Ryan (2001) when she says that they 'held each other up'.

Taylor (2000: 70) states that what flows from collective learning is 'empowerment, self-confidence and understanding' and that 'this approach values highly the lived experiences of the learners'. The tutor is critical in enabling students to make the most of the initial contact that students have with each other. Time needs to be set aside by the tutor, particularly at the beginning of any programme – not just in induction – for students to share their histories, anxieties and hopes. Students, in general, and mature students, in particular, have stories to tell of what they perceive to be their own successes and failures. It is important that they have time to reflect on their experience in the light of their new position in higher education. These stories and their sharing of them allow students to make links with others and their experiences. In this way the isolation that many mature students from under-represented groups say they feel on embarking on a higher education programme can be diminished earlier and can eventually lead to greater confidence for the individual and the group. This confidence is the basis for one of the most important aspects of learning in higher education: developing a critical faculty in relation to all that is around and within us. If tutors can set time aside in this way, it not only facilitates collective and individual learning but also delivers a strong message about how the tutor and, by implication, the institution itself values those students and their lived experiences. When Tett (2000) examined the recollected and gendered experiences of a small group of working class participants in higher education, she found that:

> Once we believe that our own story has value, and we share it with others who receive it positively, then we are likely to feel better about ourselves in ways that enable us to challenge the status quo so that our views can be seen, heard, and taken seriously. (Tett 2000: 193)

Malcolm argues that students have become 'disembodied learning mechanisms rather than . . . whole beings with community identities' (Malcolm 2000: 19). This is because time has been squeezed in the stretched academy. Tutors' teaching, administrative, curriculum management and research loads have increased. With these pressures tutors may feel like opting for more time-saving approaches in their teaching and will feel that they simply have not got time for the sharing and reflection on life stories described above, often seeing it as desirable but a luxury nonetheless. The number of students being accepted onto existing and newly developed programmes each year is generally expanding, although the corresponding resources are not put in place to meet increased demands on tutors' time.

If the academy, stretched or not, is to be a place where truth and knowledge resides is it not better to be encouraging students to ask: whose truth and whose knowledge? Concepts of truth and knowledge are not static or immutable and it is generally accepted that, at the highest levels, it is the universities that should provide new forms of knowledge and thinking. This requires: 'An open system of knowledge involves constructing knowledge from different perspectives and challenging dominant forms of knowledge' (Thomas 2001: 98). However, in the stretched academy, given what has been described here, opportunities for asking questions and challenging the traditional purveyors of knowledge have effectively diminished.

Conclusion

If all students, especially those from under-represented groups are to be provided with the appropriate support then it is necessary to look at the sort of education that is wanted for our students. At the moment, the focus is on how the mature student from under-represented groups needs to adapt to the current higher education provision – with whatever support is on offer at their institution. Tacit though it often is, the view of such mature students is that they are, in some ways, deficient in the skills and cultural experience that will enable them to make full use of a higher education. An alternative way of looking at this is to ask how higher education institutions can change so that they are inclusive and encourage participation – and achievement – in their fullest sense.

Higher education is, and will continue to be an alien place for students from under-represented groups, and the stretched academy, in many ways, makes it harder still. Thompson (2000: 10) argues that there needs to be a more democratic dialogue between academics and students and that the academy should allow the student 'to test knowledge against the template of lived experience', to produce knowledge and theory from critical reflection on experience and 'to harness the ways of understanding and acting that emerge from this process to a common and collective purpose' (Crowther et al., in Thompson 2000: 173).

Haggis (2006) and Hockings et al. (2007) acknowledge that it is those tutors who know most about their students and who seek to understand them who are more successful in creating learning environments that offer such a common and collective purpose. In order for this to be more widely achieved, however, it is necessary to confront the essential paradox of the stretched academy. This requires not only a re-consideration of who should be able to benefit from higher education but also a restructuring of resource provision within higher education. Patterns of provision need to be examined at institutional and programme level, and resources need to be increased. If such policy initiatives are pursued much more can be done in universities to make them properly inclusive for students from diverse groups and backgrounds and the stretched academy can develop teaching and learning strategies that may appear more time and staff-intensive but which will produce a more appropriate learning landscape for all students, especially those from under-represented backgrounds.

Student Intelligence: Challenging Received Wisdom in Student Surveys

9

Andy Hagyard

Introduction

Recent years have seen significant changes in the whole landscape of student surveying. Changes to the higher education quality assurance framework in the United Kingdom (HEFCE 2001) have led to greater significance being attached to student participation and representation, with an expectation that institutions will have in place robust internal mechanisms for collecting and using student feedback. Brennan and Williams (2004), in their guide to good practice, state that as greater importance is attached to student feedback, ensuring that feedback is collected effectively and used wisely becomes an increasing priority for higher education institutions.

In addition, the implementation in 2005 of an annual National Student Survey (NSS) has raised the profile of student feedback, making it a key component of the information presented to prospective students via the new 'Unistats' website (**www.unistats.co.uk**). This bold concept of a census-style survey of all final level undergraduates drew on recent experience internationally, notably in the USA and Australia. While many institutions were at best ambivalent about both the purpose and the value of the NSS, few would now deny the impact that it has had (Sullivan 2007). Not only has it highlighted areas of practice where students were clearly less satisfied with the quality of their experience, but in many cases institutions have also had to review and realign their internal processes in order to gain maximum benefit from the range of complementary internal and external sources now available to them. These can include internal feedback at module, programme, faculty or institutional level, alongside the external data provided by the NSS.

Alongside this, technological advances are leading to a rapid shift towards online surveying as the dominant mode for collecting feedback. While the ability to create electronic surveys is not new, the last few years have seen the development of a number of user-friendly systems for creating and implementing questionnaires. With ever-improving access to technology and cultural shifts towards the acceptance of online systems, it can be argued that a threshold has been crossed. The obvious benefits of electronic collection of feedback in terms of efficiency in collating, analysing and reporting data have finally outweighed concerns about validity and reliability, particularly in relation to response rates. Nevertheless, online surveying brings with it a whole set of methodological considerations.

Of course there is nothing new about including the student voice in institutional decision-making processes. Elected student representatives serve on course and subject committees and are trained to become active participants in the quality assurance of their programmes, even though there is evidence that their participation is not always very effective (Brennan and Williams 2004: 43). Within higher education generally, students are represented on committees at all levels of the institution, and there has been for many years an expectation that institutions collect student views as part of module evaluation practices. However, the introduction of the NSS marked a significant step forward, with the systematic collection of quantitative scores on student satisfaction and their public dissemination.

This chapter draws on the experience of one university within the context of national developments in student surveying. In 2003 the University of Lincoln was one of the first institutions in the United Kingdom to implement a totally online institution-wide satisfaction survey, but like many others it had to substantially review its practice in the light of the NSS. This led to the development of a concept named 'Student Intelligence', which seeks to adopt a coherent, integrated approach to student feedback within a culture where all feedback is valued and students see the act of giving feedback as part of their responsibility as members of an academic community. The chapter addresses issues of good practice in the creative collection and use of feedback, and considers methodological issues relating to online surveying. In particular it challenges two aspects of conventional wisdom; that high response rates are impossible with online surveys, and that students suffer from survey fatigue. Finally it recommends systemic and cultural solutions to ensure that student feedback is collected in a valid and reliable way as part of a continuous process of quality enhancement.

The National Student Survey

New methods of higher education quality assurance in England and Northern Ireland promised a 'lightness of touch' (HEFCE 2001), with external processes of subject review being replaced by internal processes, placing responsibility on institutions to manage their own quality assurance in a robust and transparent manner. A Task Group on Information on Quality and Standards in Higher Education chaired by Sir Ron Cooke was set up in 2001, to provide recommendations on which items of information should be made available by institutions. The final report, commonly referred to as the Cooke Report, included a recommendation that institutions should publish data 'on student satisfaction with the higher education experience' (HEFCE 2002b) covering areas such as teaching quality, learning resources, academic support, pastoral care and assessment arrangements. They also specifically recommended that two particular aspects of student satisfaction should be published: feedback from recent graduates collected through a national survey, and feedback from current students collected through the institutions' own surveys.

Ultimately, only the first of these recommendations appeared in the resulting White Paper (DfES 2003). Institutions were no longer required to publish the results of internal surveys, amidst concerns that this would interfere with the primary purpose of local feedback, namely the enhancement of teaching quality. However, the recommendation for a national survey was taken forward to become the NSS, piloted in 2004 and implemented nationally in 2005.

The NSS had three specified aims: to help inform the choices of prospective students, to contribute to public accountability and to provide useful data for institutions to use in their enhancement activities (HEA 2007). In designing the first NSS, the steering group drew heavily on the Course Experience Questionnaire (CEQ) which had been in operation in Australia for several years and was considered to be a proven instrument with a sound theory-base (HEA 2007). The only methodological departure was in its timing. While the CEQ is administered alongside the Graduate Destinations Survey in Australia to the previous year's graduates, concerns about the need for high response rates to ensure the credibility of the NSS led to its redesign as a survey of students in their final year of study and therefore still captive and easily accessible within their institutions and through institutional email addresses.

While commonly referred to as questions, the NSS actually consists of 22 statements to which the respondent is invited to express the level of their agreement on a five point Likert scale from 1 (definitely disagree) to 5 (definitely agree). The first 21 statements concern specific aspects of the student experience, such as 'Staff are good at explaining things' and 'Feedback on my work has been prompt', and are grouped into six broad topic areas known as 'scales'. These are 'The teaching on my course', 'Assessment and feedback',

'Academic support', 'Organisation and management', 'Learning resources' and 'Personal development'. The 22nd statement concerns overall satisfaction with the course, and it is this score which is most commonly used for direct comparisons and the creation of league tables. Finally, there are two open comment boxes for additional positive and negative comments about the course. Results are expressed either as an arithmetic mean of the responses, or as a percentage of students agreeing or disagreeing with the statement. The 22 statements have remained unchanged through the first four years of the NSS, although additional optional scales have been made available to institutions on request.

Reactions to the National Student Survey

Prior to the introduction of the NSS there was a degree of ambivalence within the sector as to the usefulness and validity of the survey. In particular, it was widely felt that the aim of accountability would directly conflict with the secondary objective of enhancement. Brennan and Williams (2004) stress the need for clarity of purpose in collecting feedback, particularly in terms of differentiating between external quality assurance and internal quality enhancement. Harvey (2003a) argued strongly against the survey, describing it as an 'unacceptable intrusion into university life that will damage existing improvement processes based on internal explorations of student satisfaction'. He went on to claim that: 'the proposed survey...will clash with these important internal processes, also scheduled for the spring term. The result will be low response rates on one or probably both surveys' (Harvey 2003a).

Prosser (2005) also argued that the results of surveys should not be used to form league tables, and that the use of student surveys as satisfaction ratings is not helpful in attempting to improve students' experiences of learning. Survey results are known to correlate with students' experiences of learning and their own approaches to study. Therefore, rather than changing teaching practice, it is often more productive to influence student perceptions, and bring their experiences into line with the way the curriculum is delivered.

Further concerns over the NSS were raised once it became apparent that information from some of the country's leading research-based institutions would not be included in the 2005 results, due to poor response rates. Student-led campaigns and boycotts meant that the Universities of Oxford,

Cambridge and Warwick in particular did not reach the 50 per cent response threshold needed for publication.

However, many of the worst fears have not been realized. Even in its first year the NSS achieved a response rate in excess of 60 per cent, a figure which has been maintained ever since. 131 out of 141 eligible institutions achieved the 50 per cent publication threshold in 2005, and by 2007 the total had risen to 144, with the notable inclusions of the Universities of Oxford and Warwick. Most tellingly, a number of Scottish universities have voluntarily opted into the NSS, despite the fact that Scotland has its own Quality Enhancement Framework. Richardson (2005) in his assessment of the survey concludes that the quality of responses is very high, with few missing answers and very little evidence of 'yea-saying', where respondents simply give the same answer to every question without thinking about the meaning.

There remain nonetheless concerns about the NSS. League tables are of course popular with those who perform well but their validity can be questioned, especially when the differences between institutions are in many cases not statistically significant. Year on year improvements in satisfaction may be less to do with genuine enhancements than strategic behaviour on the part of students. While some institutions have been reprimanded for overtly suggesting this to students (Sanders 2006; Attwood 2008), there is a general realization that it is in students' own interest, in terms of the value of their degree, for their institutions to perform well.

There is understandable ambivalence towards the uses of NSS data in constructing league tables, both at subject and institutional level. Yet what is undeniable is the value of a dataset containing the views of some 170,000 students, including qualitative comments on their experience. This gives unprecedented scope for research into student perceptions of their experience, particularly in terms of variations between different groups. Surridge's (2006, 2007) analysis provides fascinating insight into students' views, highlighting for example the impact of age and ethnicity on satisfaction.

For individual institutions, the bitter pill of external accountability has been softened by access to detailed data, above and beyond what is available publicly. This data, made available on a protected basis through the NSS dissemination website, provides information on programmes of study which did not have sufficient numbers for publication. It also contains data on aspects such as ethnicity, age, gender and socio-economic background as well as the qualitative comments which provide valuable insight into some of the causes of variation in scores. Finally, it allows for a degree of benchmarking against other institutions, so that genuine like-for-like comparisons can be made.

Experience at the University of Lincoln

Like many institutions, the University of Lincoln was quick to realize that this data could usefully serve to complement existing data from internal surveys, rather than be seen as duplicating it. Indeed the triangulation of data served as an additional check of validity, particularly in areas where either the NSS or the internal survey had suffered from low response rates. In order to maximize the enhancement potential of the NSS, the internal processes that had been used by the University for the previous three years were redesigned in 2006 to align in both content and methodology with the NSS and were streamlined to avoid duplication.

NSS results were disaggregated by programme and systematically circulated to heads of department, along with the qualitative comments from the dissemination site. Faculties and service departments were then required to develop action plans to address any issues identified. Progress against these action plans was monitored through the University's committee structure.

However, detailed analysis of students' comments from both the NSS and internal surveys consistently revealed great variability in the student experience, with students reporting difficulty in awarding a single score for such a diverse range:

> Occasionally, there will be one tutor who has difficulty communicating the information in a lecture and this lets the rest of the tutors down who are brilliant.
>
> Some of the modules are very hard going and almost appear irrelevant to the overall outcome of the degree.
>
> I have experienced late results and feedback from one module and I'm not happy with the lack of feedback.

It became increasingly clear that effective use of feedback would require a breakdown at the level of individual modules, so that specific aspects could be targeted for improvement and aspects of good practice identified for broader dissemination. This is consistent with Harvey's (2003b) recommendation in his report to HEFCE that student feedback should be available for analysis at a number of levels: individual module, programme of study, school or faculty, and institution.

Module level feedback has been routinely collected for many years within the University of Lincoln, as part of standard monitoring processes. However, responsibility for designing, administering, analysing and reporting on the process has previously been devolved to faculties, since it has been generally accepted as good practice nationally that feedback instruments should recognize disciplinary variations and that standard questionnaires are not appropriate (Harvey 2003b).

The impact of the NSS radically changed thinking in this area. The need for internal module-level feedback to complement the wealth of data coming from the NSS became the more pressing concern, overriding the conflicting desire for local flexibility. The University's core executive decided to implement a centralized and standardized module evaluation system, which would allow greater scope for comparisons and benchmarking both within and beyond the institution. For example, consistency of methodology would enable like-for-like comparisons within and between subject areas, while alignment with the NSS would then allow these scores to be benchmarked against sector scores.

Once this aim was agreed, subsequent discussion focused particularly on the feedback instrument to be developed, and specifically on the mode. While faculties are encouraged to use a range of formal and informal mechanisms for collecting feedback, the traditional paper-based, end-of-module questionnaire, distributed and completed in lecture time, has remained the dominant method. The potential efficiency gains from electronic surveying are clear, but early pilots were consistently plagued by low response rates. (Brennan and Williams 2004: 40–1, CRQ 2006). Speculation as to the causes varied (Harvey 2003b; CRQ 2006), citing access to technology, concerns regarding confidentiality and difficulties in maintaining reliable email contact, among others. Motivation is also a key factor, as an email is much easier to ignore than a lecturer standing by a door. Yet high response rates obtained through a degree of coercion may well be counter-productive if we aim to encourage thoughtful and reflective feedback from students on their experience, rather than mechanistic box-ticking to satisfy procedural requirements. After much debate and consideration of a range of alternatives, it was decided to pilot a fully online module evaluation system with a small number of selected modules from across the institution. The survey instrument was designed to align with the NSS in terms of methodology, using the same five-point Likert scale to express agreement or disagreement with a number of statements. The set of questions was however reduced and adapted to be relevant to evaluation of an individual module. As in the NSS, two open comment boxes were included for positive and negative additional comments.

The broad aims of the pilot were to assess the appropriateness of the survey instrument and to test a number of processes in its administration, analysis and reporting. However, one very specific aim was to demonstrate whether or not a fully online system could generate satisfactory response rates, and to assess the quality of these responses. For the purposes of the pilot, and in line with NSS methodology, 50 per cent was agreed as the acceptable response rate for valid results. The pilot used a commercial online survey design tool, chosen for its ease of use and its inclusion of key features such as the creation of personalized emails and automatic reminders to non-respondents. However, the system itself was not being evaluated, as it was recognized that a full-scale implementation would require investment in a more sophisticated product.

A small group of five modules was selected to represent all faculties at different levels, with modules ranging in size from 31 to 208 students, and with varying cultures in terms of the integration of electronic delivery methods. Prior to the pilot, programme leaders were contacted individually to explain the purpose of the pilot, and to ask them to subsequently explain and promote the survey to their students. In particular they were asked to remind students to consult their university email account, which would be used to provide access to the survey. The pilot was timed to take place after the initial stages of the NSS, and was therefore conducted in March 2007.

Evaluation of the pilot module evaluation scheme

Each module in the pilot achieved the target response rate of 50 per cent, with one exception which received responses from 46 per cent of students. This was achieved by sending an individualized email to each student containing the link to the survey, followed by a reminder sent one week later to non-respondents. The ability to send reminders appears critical in this success, with more students actually responding to the second invitation than the first one. Of 408 students included in the pilot, only ten explicitly opted out of the survey, even though the email contained a clear link to do this.

Of the students who responded, over half also supplied additional comments in at least one, and typically both, of the comment boxes. These comments were generally full paragraphs of constructive comments, with no abusive remarks and very few of the one-line statements typical of paper-based evaluations. There was a good mix of positive remarks and suggested improvements. The mean time for completion of the survey can be calculated as two minutes for those who did not provide additional comments and five minutes for those who did.

One module in particular stood out as having an exceptionally high and swift response rate, with 40 per cent responding within two days of the initial email and 65 per cent after one reminder. On investigation, this success appeared to be a direct result of the programme leader addressing the students directly to explain the purpose of the survey and present it in positive terms.

The success of the pilot led the University's Teaching and Learning Development Committee to conclude that an online system could achieve both satisfactory response rates and better quality comments than existing processes, provided that a number of systemic and cultural elements were in place. On a technical level these included the ability of the system to generate automatic reminders for non-respondents. Positive promotion by staff is critical to the establishment of a feedback culture, as is the transparent communication of purpose, results and actions. The committee recommended the procurement of a commercial product which was fit for purpose, and a system that met the University's requirements was installed in 2007 ready for implementation during 2008. One of the key features of this system is its ability to link directly to the University's student management system, thereby allowing a whole range of surveys to be designed and administered to targeted groups of students in a strategically managed way. While the pilot was conducted by the Teaching and Learning Development Office (TLDO), it was agreed that ultimate responsibility for managing the system should lie with the Academic Registry, although the TLDO would continue to advise on the effective use of feedback for enhancement purposes.

Key issues in online surveying

Aside from the issue of response rate, there is evidence that the experience of providing feedback electronically is qualitatively different to other modes. The respondent is able to choose the time and place for completion, can take as long as they like and is free from the pressure or influence of any third party. The local evidence strongly suggests that this leads to better quality responses, as detailed above. While survey fatigue has emerged as a commonly cited concern, it tends to occur when students are presented with a plethora of surveys, with conflicting or unclear purposes, and with no clear feedback to students or any evidence of changes made as a result. Conversely, there has been no evidence of fatigue when surveys are presented as part of a well-managed feedback system, as represented by Brennan and Williams' feedback cycle (2004: 7). Indeed a member of the University's Student Union Executive expressed the view of many students, saying that she was 'happy to complete as many surveys as necessary as long the results were used effectively'.

Driven by its concern to maximize response rates, the NSS has consistently adopted a multi-modal approach, with an online phase being followed by a postal phase, and finally a telephone phase. This provides a unique opportunity to compare responses by mode: Surridge's analysis (2006, 2007) demonstrates clearly that scores from telephone respondents are significantly higher than other modes, once all other factors are taken into account. The causes of this are open to speculation, whether they are due to the influence of talking to a third party as opposed to the anonymity of using a computer, or whether the response to an aural prompt is different to choosing an option on a visual five-point Likert scale. Whatever the causes, there is a compelling case for surveys to stick consistently to a single response mode, and comparisons between results derived from different methods need to be treated with some caution.

In fact the experience of the NSS confirms the rapid shift towards online surveying as the dominant mode. In 2005, 31 per cent of all responses were received online, significantly fewer than the number of telephone respondents. This translates into an overall response rate to the initial online survey of 18.7 per cent. By 2006 this had increased to 25 per cent, and an accompanying relaxation of repeat telephone calls meant that online responses accounted for 44 per cent of the total. While at the time of writing national figures are not yet available for 2007, there is evidence that the trend has continued. The University of Lincoln achieved an online response rate of 43 per cent in 2007, rising to 45 per cent in 2008, within a total response rate of 66 per cent.

High response rates are clearly important, particularly in establishing the credibility of the survey, yet in pure methodological terms the response rate is less important than the representativeness of the sample. Even a 60 per cent rate will not produce valid results if the remaining 40 per cent have substantially different characteristics. This is one of the reasons why in-class evaluation can be seen as flawed, as it can be reasonably assumed that non-attendees will have different perceptions of their experience. Surridge's (2006) analysis demonstrates marginal differences between respondents according to mode, particularly in relation to dyslexic students, who prefer to respond by telephone. However, she concludes that 'there is good reason to be confident that the sample of students that did respond to the survey was representative of the student population (Surridge 2006: 25). However, she also claims that the removal of telephone responses could have potentially damaging effects on response rates and argues that 'it would be to the detriment of the survey if telephone were not an available mode of response' (Surridge 2006: 25). In the light of the more recent experience detailed above, this particular piece of received wisdom needs to be challenged. While there may be a case for providing alternative modes for specific groups of students, the clear discrepancy in results between modes coupled with the evidence of the high response rates that are achievable with online surveys, suggests that institutions should now be prepared to come to terms with adopting wholly online methods.

A final issue in online surveying is that of anonymity and confidentiality. Online surveys clearly cannot pretend to be anonymous when respondents are linked to their student record and when reminders are sent to non-respondents. Instead, the University of Lincoln has always stressed the confidentiality of reporting, ensuring that results are reported in such a way that no individual can be identified. In practice, this has not once been raised as a concern by students in five years of conducting online surveys.

Student Intelligence

The term 'Student Intelligence' has been coined within the University of Lincoln to refer to a holistic approach to the collection and effective use of student feedback. This includes the systematic use of NSS data alongside data from internal surveys and the implementation of a centralized module evaluation system. Equally it is important to invite and incorporate feedback from other formal and informal sources, such as student representation.

Alongside the development of structures and system, it is perhaps even more important to promote a culture where feedback is valued both by staff and students. As Sullivan says, the answer to the question of the value of the

NSS, or indeed other feedback mechanism, is that it depends on the culture of the institution. 'Command and control cultures will cause the NSS to fail; cultures of mutual support will keep moving forward' (Sullivan 2007: 22).

It is particularly important in this respect to reassure staff that feedback systems are not simply intended as a way of identifying and targeting under-performing staff. The University has deliberately stopped short of using online systems to evaluate individual staff for precisely this reason, although inevitably it can be easy to identify staff teaching small modules. For this reason there is a great deal of sensitivity around the reporting of qualitative comments. While they are sanitized for abusive or personal comments, there may inevitably remain valid comments which will make uncomfortable reading for a tutor or module co-ordinator. It is therefore important that individual comments are published on a restricted basis, for example to programme leaders and tutors, and issues handled as part of a well-managed process of continuing professional development. Nevertheless, systematic qualitative analysis of comments should also be carried out centrally as they carry powerful explanatory information, shedding light on the issues raised through the quantitative scores.

Student motivation is clearly critical to the success of any feedback system, and it is important to establish a culture where students view the act of giving feedback as part of their responsibility as a member of the academic community. It is increasingly common for student participation in surveys to be encouraged by attractive prizes or other incentives. However, it could be argued that this sends out the wrong message, encouraging engagement at a superficial level purely motivated by potential reward. Nor is there much evidence that these inducements have any impact; the NSS manages to achieve excellent response rates without any systematic form of incentive. The most obvious motivation is for students to see tangible improvements as a result of their feedback, and institutions must ensure that attention is paid to all stages of the 'feedback cycle' (Brennan and Williams 2004), particularly in terms of the publication and dissemination of results. Again, online systems offer considerable advantages in systematically providing students with the results of surveys and actions to be taken. While the timing of module evaluations generally precludes any possibility of students witnessing improvements resulting directly from their own feedback, there are many examples of good practice, whereby feedback on the previous year's evaluation is routinely included in module handbooks.

It is, however, important to stress that the process of implementing Student Intelligence is still in its infancy. While it is grounded in established good practice, it is still too early to assess the extent to which it can result in genuine enhancements. Many process issues around the timing of surveys and the release of results need to be resolved during its first full year of operation. Early indications suggest that the qualitative comments will be particularly useful both at local level to inform curriculum and personal development, and as evidence to inform institutional research into the student experience.

Conclusion

The landscape of student surveying has shifted dramatically in recent years. National quality assurance mechanisms place greater emphasis on the student voice, and technological advances make it increasingly easy not only to collect student feedback, but also to make this information available to prospective students in a manner intended to inform their choice. Whatever UK higher education institutions may think of the National Student Survey they cannot ignore it, nor deny the significant impact that it has had. The University of Lincoln will not be the only institution feeling compelled to review its internal feedback mechanisms and to align them with the dominant methodology of the NSS.

The challenge for institutions is to ensure that the pressures of public accountability and the spectre of league tables do not distract them from the potential of using student feedback to inform genuine enhancement of the student experience. NSS data, used alongside internal sources, provides a powerful tool to gain real insight into students' views on their experience and bring about genuine enhancements.

There are aspects of received wisdom that need to be challenged, however. The first of these is the view which, at least until recently, was widely held: that online surveying cannot produce response rates adequate enough to ensure valid and reliable results. As online systems become increasingly sophisticated and user-friendly, there is ample evidence that this is no longer the case. Given the changing nature of the student body which, as Watling highlighted in Chapter 7, is increasingly accustomed to using interactive web-based technology, this is perhaps not surprising. Indeed online surveying would appear to have significant benefits, both in terms of efficiency and also of the quality of feedback received. Furthermore, significant variations in results from differing modes of response suggest that surveys should not employ multi-modal collection systems, except in specific circumstances, in order to ensure the validity of their results.

Second, this chapter challenges the view that students suffer from survey fatigue. It is certainly true that students will become disillusioned and apathetic when faced with a multitude of poorly designed surveys with no clear purpose and little indication of what actions are taken as a result. Conversely, students will on the whole be happy to contribute to a well-designed survey when they have clear information about its purpose and can see evidence that real enhancements can occur as a result.

The keys to effective practice in collecting feedback are partly systemic and partly cultural. Most importantly, universities need to establish a culture where feedback is valued and acted upon, and where students view the act of giving feedback as part of their responsibility as a member of an academic community. On average students are expected to spend 120 hours of study on each module. Is it really too much to expect them to spend an additional two to five minutes contributing to its continuing improvement?

The Student as Producer: Reinventing the Student Experience in Higher Education

10

Mike Neary and Joss Winn

Introduction

The university is one of the great success stories of the twentieth century, with numbers of students growing exponentially in the last fifty years. There are now more than 600 million students around the world, with no signs of this expansion slowing down (Wolf 2002). And yet, academics have argued that this success has come at a cost, with the intellectual and scientific mission of the university undermined by the way in which universities have allowed themselves to be redesigned according to the logic of market economics (Evans 2004).

Since the 1980s, universities, in response to government pressure, have become more business-like and enterprising to take advantage of the 'opportunities' presented by the so-called global 'knowledge economy' and 'information society' (Levidow 2002; Wright 2004). This process of corporatization of higher education is extended through the increasing regularization and intensification of the academic labour processes (Nelson and Watt 2003; De Angelis and Harvie 2006) and the reconfiguration of the student as consumer (Boden and Epstein 2006). The process of the student as consumer is driven by both the intensification and casualization of the graduate labour market which demands not only that students pay undivided attention to their employability, but also, at the same time, prepare themselves for periods of under-employability, un-employability, student poverty and debt (Bonefeld 1995; TUC-NUS 2006; Warmington 2007).

This controversial notion of student as consumer is much discussed in academic circles, but what is less well debated is the extent to which the basis of student life might be rearranged within higher education. The point of this re-arrangement would be to reconstruct the student as producer: undergraduate students working in collaboration with academics to create work of social importance that is full of academic content and value, while at the same time reinvigorating the university beyond the logic of market economics.

The nature and purpose of the university

The point at which we begin to reconstruct the student as producer begins with what is understood as the real nature or purpose of the university. There is no longer any consensus about the *idea* (Newman 1853) or the *uses* (Kerr 1963) of the university, if indeed there ever was.

While there may be no general agreement about its nature, it is clear that what constitutes the core activity of the university is teaching and research. The relationship between these two aspects of higher education is not straightforward; indeed higher education is characterized by the severe imbalance between teaching and research, leading to what has been called an 'apartheid' between student and teacher (Brew 2006). However, it is precisely this dysfunctionality that provides the catalyst for rethinking the relationship between research and teaching in a way that can construct a framework upon which to rebalance the basis of student life, providing the space to ask fundamental questions about the purposes of higher education (Brew 2006: 3).

This rationale for the relationship between teaching and research had already been established in European conventions through the *Magna Charta Universitatum*. In 1988, Rectors of European Universities gathered in Bologna and signed the *Magna Charta Universitatum* (EUA 1988) in which, as part of a wider debate about the role of the university in contemporary society, they set out the framework for an integrated system of European higher education.

The *Charta* set out some fundamental principles about the future of higher education in Europe, as well as outlining the means by which these fundamental principles could be achieved. Key to all of this was the issue of academic freedom for tutors and students and that central to the issue of academic freedom was the relationship between teaching and research. The principles included the assertion that to meet the needs of the world around it, research and teaching must be morally and intellectually independent of all political authority and economic power. Teaching and research in universities must be inseparable if tuition is not to lag behind changing needs, the demands of society and advances in scientific knowledge.

Cleary, there is more at stake than teaching students research skills. What is at issue is the recovery or the continuation of the university as a liberal humanist institution, based on some notion of the 'true university' and the 'public good'.

At around the same period in the US, Ernest Boyer was pointing out the imbalance between research and teaching and arguing for a reconfiguration of teaching and research, with teaching recognized as an important and fundamental part of academic life. Boyer provided a framework on which to consider the relationship between teaching and research, and was concerned with reinventing the relationship between teaching and learning in higher education in the US: 'The most important obligation now confronting colleges and universities is to break out of the tired old teaching versus research debate and define in more creative ways what it means to be a scholar' (Boyer 1990: xii).

Boyer encapsulated this debate with the creation of four categories of what he referred to as 'scholarship': the scholarship of discovery – research; the scholarship of integration – interdisciplinary connections; the scholarship of application and engagement – knowledge applied in the wider community; and the scholarship of teaching – research and evaluation of one's own teaching (Boyer 1990). The Boyer Commission, established in his name, set out to create its own *Magna Charta* for students in the form of an Academic Bill of Rights, which included the commitment for every university to provide 'opportunities to learn through enquiry rather than simple transmission of knowledge' (Boyer Commission 1999).

The origins of these versions of the liberal humanist university are found in the formulation that underpinned the framework for the first modern European university, the Friedrich Wilhelms University of Berlin founded in 1810. Inspired by the writings of Wilhelm Humboldt, Berlin University was organized around the principle of maintaining a close relationship between research and teaching.

In Humboldt's model (1810) of what he referred to as 'organic scholarship', the simple transmission of knowledge through lectures would be abandoned, with teaching taking place solely in seminars. Students were to be directly involved in the speculative thinking of their tutors, in a Socratic dialogue and in close contact, without strictly planned courses and curricula. Students should work in research communities with time for thinking and without any practical obligations.

Humboldt argued this in terms of academic freedom, not only between the student and their teacher, but in terms of the relationship between the university and the state. Humboldt's point was that in guaranteeing the academic freedom of the university, the state itself is regenerated by the way in which the university promotes and preserves the culture of the nation. In so doing, what he described as a 'Culture State' is established, which includes a genuinely cultured population who are trained to act as independent and autonomous citizens.

Humboldt's model was quickly overwhelmed by what he feared most: the rise of industrial capitalism and the subsumption of the 'Culture State' by the 'Commercial State', to which the university became increasingly tied through government and private sector research contracts in a process where teaching became not only detached from research, but a subordinate and less profitable activity (Knoll and Siebert 1967).

Policy and practice in teaching and research

Despite the pre-eminence of the research agenda, the nature of the core activities of higher education makes it very difficult to detach research from teaching. Indeed, the importance of maintaining research in the undergraduate curriculum was recognized in the report by the Robbins Committee on Higher Education (1963): 'there is no borderline between teaching and research; they are complementary and overlapping activities' (Committee on Higher Education 1963: 181–2), even if the chance to do research was to be made available only to the best students in the best universities (Committee on Higher Education 1963).

A similar approach based on research in the undergraduate curriculum, although aimed at a very different kind of student, was developed in 1974 at North East London Polytechnic as a programme of 'independent study'. The essential difference between such independent study programmes and Robbins' ideas for providing research in the undergraduate curriculum was that the independent study programme was designed in a way that embodied 'left-wing' ideals and made for 'a completely different approach to Higher Education' – to meet the needs of the new type of student (Pratt 1997: 138).

This debate about the appropriateness of research in non-research intensive universities was reflected in the approach advocated by the White Paper on Higher Education (DfES 2003) for 'teaching only universities'. However, in the face of reasoned opposition, there was an acknowledgement by the government of the need for the post-1992 universities to develop 'research informed teaching environments' (DfES 2003; Healey et al. forthcoming).

The creation of a research environment that included undergraduate students has been encouraged by the ways in which leading US universities are linking undergraduate teaching and research. Stanford and Massachusetts Institute of Technology, most notably, have developed their own undergraduate research programmes, known generally as Undergraduate Research Opportunity Programmes. The point of these programmes is that undergraduate students work in collaboration with academics on real research projects, presenting their findings at conferences and authoring joint papers. In the United Kingdom, the lead in creating this kind of research environment for undergraduate students was taken by University of Warwick and Imperial College, London, although a number of other institutions have now followed suit. Following the success of these schemes the Higher Education Academy and the Scottish Executive Enhancement Committee have made the establishment of links between research and teaching in undergraduate programmes a key priority.

As the issue of connections between research and teaching has climbed higher up the higher education agenda the amount of research into this area has increased. One of the most unsettling conclusions was that the links between teaching and research are not nearly so well established as had been imagined (Hattie and Marsh 1996). While students enjoyed being involved with a research intensive university their actual experiences were not always positive (Zamorski 2002).

However with the closer engagement between research and teaching, where students are engaged in research-like and research-related activities, the results become much more positive. A number of powerful arguments emerge as to why and how research-based teaching and learning can raise the level and quality of teaching and learning in higher education. These include the notion that research-based learning effectively develops critical academic and evaluative skills that are used to support problem-based and inquiry-based learning and to raise the level of more traditional project work (Wieman 2004). This style of learning also equips students to continue learning after tertiary study, making links to the lifelong-learning agenda (Brew 2006). Other points in favour of research-based learning are that it encourages students to construct knowledge through increasing participation within different communities of practice (Cole 1990; Scribner 1985); this can be set against the positivist model of teaching, where faculty experts are transmitters of knowledge to the passive student recipient. It is also argued that this model of research-based learning exemplifies a social-constructivist view of learning (Vygotsky 1962, 1978; Bruner 1986; Barr and Tagg 1995).

As well as encouraging participation and retention at the same time as 'elevating degree aspirations' and degree completion, research-based learning increases the likelihood that students will decide to go on to postgraduate work (Pascarella and Terenzini 2005). Moreover, recent research points to the fact that research-based learning is an attractive option for students across all ages and agendas, and particularly among mature and part-time students (Smith and Rust 2007).

Centres for Excellence in Teaching and Learning (CETLs)

In the United Kingdom, some of the most significant progress in linking teaching and research has been achieved by the CETLs that were set up in 2005 to promote research and enquiry-based learning. These include the Centre for Inquiry-Based Learning in the Arts and Social Sciences at Sheffield University (**www.shef.ac.uk/cilass**) which is providing rich evidence of the value of inquiry-based learning across a wide range of disciplines, from the first year of undergraduate study to taught Master's level. Part of their work is designing experimental teaching spaces: 'collaboratories' to encourage engagement between teachers and students. The Centre for Applied Undergraduate Research Skills at the University of Reading (**www.engageinresearch.ac.uk**) has established 'Engage', an interactive research resource for undergraduate bioscience students. At Sheffield Hallam (**extra.shu.ac.uk/cetl/cplahome.html**), students involved with the Centre for Promoting Learner Autonomy take responsibility for their learning and work in partnership with tutors and other students. This involves high levels of trust and risk taking by all concerned.

The work done by these CETLs contributes to the development of the research-based teaching agenda, but what these CETLs do not do is explicitly link the developments in teaching and learning with the debate about the real nature or the idea of the university.

The Reinvention Centre for Undergraduate Research (www.warwick/ac.uk/go/reinvention), a collaborative CETL based in the Sociology department at the University of Warwick and the School of the Built Environment at Oxford Brookes, has attempted to connect the developments in teaching and learning with the debate about the future of the university (Neary et al. 2007).

The work of the Reinvention Centre is informed by the most progressive discourses of teaching and learning, such as Boyer – from whose Reinvention Commission the centre gets its name – in dialogue and debate with social science critical traditions. The result is a more radical agenda than is normally found in mainstream teaching and learning activity, but one that is grounded in the traditions of its own subject areas. The framework within which the Reinvention Centre defines its activity within the CETL programme is one of Skelton's excellence paradigms: the concept of 'critical excellence' (Skelton 2005).

The critical approach to excellence, as defined by the Reinvention Centre, sees institutional change as the outcome of conflict and struggle, forming part of a much wider social, political and economic context beyond the institution. This approach, which can claim much of its legitimacy from the student protests in 1968, and the progressive forms of teaching and learning that developed out of these protests, aims to radically democratize the process of knowledge production at the level of society. For this critical model, institutional and social change is not simply the product of incremental policy changes, strategic planning or teaching innovation, but emerges out of much wider social, political and economic processes, resulting in 'paradigm shifts' (Kuhn 1970) and revolutionary transformations in the practice of teaching and learning.

Critical in this sense does not mean 'negative judgements', but rather, negative dialectics (Adorno 1966) – the positive power of negative thinking (Fuller 2005), or the awareness of the progressive possibilities that are inherent in even the most contradictory and dysfunctional contexts. This approach is inspired by the Frankfurt School including, among others, the work of Walter Benjamin, one of the most creative modern Marxist thinkers.

In *Life of Students*, Benjamin writes about the separated nature of higher education, as 'a gigantic game of hide and seek in which students and teachers, each in his or her own unified identity, constantly push past one another without ever seeing one another' (Benjamin 1915: 39). Even in the early twentieth century, Benjamin was critical of the lecture and seminar formats:

> The most striking and painful aspect of the university is the mechanical reaction of the students as they listen to a lecture [and seminars which] mainly rely on the lecture format, and it makes little difference whether the speakers are teachers or students. (Benjamin 1915: 42)

Benjamin had his own version of student as producer, referring back to the origins of the Humboldtian university:

> The organisation of the university has ceased to be grounded in the productivity of its students, as its founders had envisaged. They thought of students as teachers and learners at the same time; as teachers because productivity implies complete autonomy, with their minds fixed on science instead of the instructors' personality. (Benjamin 1915: 42)

By the 1930s, in an article entitled 'Author as Producer', Benjamin extended these ideas of productive autonomy between students and teachers and looked beyond the university to include relationships between authors and their readers. The purpose of these connections was to find ways in which intellectuals might engage with matters of serious social concern in practices that lay beyond simply being committed to an issue, or through disengaged academic forms of solidarity.

Benjamin argued that intellectual work could only be politically progressive if it satisfied two criteria. First, it must be of high quality, and second, it must seek actively to intervene in 'the living context of social relations', what Benjamin referred to as the 'organising function', in ways that seek to create progressive social transformation:

> [For] . . . the author who has reflected deeply on the conditions of present day production . . . His work will never be merely work on products but always, at the same time, work on the means of production. In other words his products must have, over and above their character as works, an organizing function. (Benjamin 1934: 777)

The organizing function within which Benjamin was writing was the social relations of capitalist production, defined through the logic of waged labour and private property. For Benjamin, the imperatives of capitalist production had led to the horrors of Bolshevism and Fascism. Therefore, any alternative form of the organizing principle must be antithetical to these extreme types of political systems and be set up on the basis of democracy, collectivism, respective for legitimate authority, mutuality and social justice.

Benjamin offered examples of this type of organizing principle from the most progressive forms of political art: Dada, Brecht's Epic Theatre and experimental Russian avant-garde art. Key to these art forms was involving the reader and spectator in the process of production: not only are they the producers of artistic content, but collaborators of their own social world; the subjects rather than objects of history.

> What matters is the exemplary character of production, which is able, first, to induce other producers to produce, and, second, to put an improved apparatus at their disposal. And this apparatus is better, the more consumers it is able to turn into producers – that is, readers or spectators, into collaborators. (Benjamin 1934: 777)

In the context of the modern university, the organizing function is the law of market economics, redefined in the contemporary period as the neo-liberal university. While the dangers that defined Benjamin's world have been overcome, the risk of the re-emergence of regressive political movements has not been eradicated and new risks and possible catastrophes have emerged that place human society in peril. The question remains as to the extent to which market economics is implicated in these social, political and economic hazards and what kind of alternative organizing principles might be invented as progressive alternatives.

The Reinvention Centre offers no simple solutions to these questions; rather, following Benjamin, it pays attention to the quality of its academic outputs and considers its position in relation to the organizational function of the university and the social, economic and political context from which it is derived. Taking its cue from Benjamin's 'Author as Producer', the Reinvention Centre has challenged the consumerist discourse that pervades the student experience by inventing the concept of the student as producer. Building on work that is already ongoing in the academy and in debate with colleagues working in the most progressive liberal humanist traditions, the Reinvention Centre has been pushing the idea of the student as producer to the limits of its critical potential, as reflected in the nature and character of its work with students (**www.warwick.ac.uk/go/reinvention**). This work has included publishing an edited collection of student work, developing an online undergraduate student journal and writing and producing films with students (Neary et al. 2007).

General intellect

In the most recent period progressive Marxist writing on universities has focused on the notion of the 'general intellect'. The general intellect, Marx argued, is the inventive, creative force of capitalism.

> Nature builds no machines, no locomotives, railways, electric telegraphs, self-acting mules etc. These are products of human industry: natural material

transformed into organs of the human will over nature, or of human participation in nature. They are organs of the human brain, created by the human hand: the power of knowledge, objectified. The development of fixed capital indicates to what degree general social knowledge has become a direct force of production, and to what degree, hence, the conditions of the process of social life itself have come under the control of the general intellect and been transformed in accordance with it. (Marx 1993: 706)

Dyer-Witheford has shown that Marx's notion of the general intellect is mobilized by the automation of machinery and the development of transportation and communication networks integrated into the 'world market' (Dyer-Witheford 1999: 484). This mobilization of the general intellect increasingly subordinates and eliminates the need for human labour and therefore the very thing on which capitalist expansiveness is based. Furthermore, Marx argued that technoscientific development which relies on the general intellect is increasingly a social, co-operative endeavour. As we come to realize this, the organizing principles on which capitalist production is based, wage labour and private ownership, become increasingly irrelevant.

Automation and socialisation together create the possibility of – and necessity for – dispensing with wage labour and private ownership. In the era of general intellect 'Capital thus works towards its own dissolution as the form dominating production'. (Dyer-Witheford 1999: 485)

However, as capitalism continues to thrive on technological innovation and development, Marx's general intellect is found to be not 'general' at all but, rather, structured and hierarchical. Knowledge remains contained, under control and restricted to the privileged under the logic of the information society and the knowledge economy. The point and the problem is how to generalize and socialize Marx's general intellect in order to resist what Noble argues is, within the university context, the 'systematic conversion of intellectual activity into intellectual capital, and, hence, intellectual property' (Noble 1998). In order to generalize the general intellect, the issue becomes not mass education but the notion of 'mass intellectuality' (Virno 1996; Virno and Hardt 1996; Hardt and Negri 2000).

Dyer-Witheford shows that what Marx defined as the 'general intellect' is now better understood as the 'mass intellect'. This is the social body of knowledge, modes of communication and co-operation and even ethical preoccupations which both supports *and* transgresses the operation of a high-tech economy. It is not knowledge created by and contained within the university, but is the 'general social knowledge' embodied by and increasingly available to all of us. The quintessential expression of this general social knowledge or 'mass intellect' is, Dyer-Witheford argues, the internet:

> The development of this extraordinarily powerful technology has in fact depended on a mass of informal, innovatory, intellectual activity – 'hacking' – on whose creativity commerce constantly draws even as it criminalizes it. It was precisely out of capital's inability to contain such activity that there emerged the astounding growth of the Internet. This is surely the quintessential institution of 'general intellect'. For, despite all the admitted banalities and exclusivities of Internet practice, one at moments glimpses in its global exchanges what seems like the formation of a polycentric, communicatively-connected, collective intelligence. (Dyer-Witheford 1999: 498)

Mass intellectuality thrives on the porosity of the internet, leaking into emerging spaces and flowing against capital's networks, transgressing intellectual property on an epidemic scale.

For the progressive academic and student producer, a model for an alternative organizing principle exists in the various forms of Free Culture, a movement defined by the work of Lawrence Lessig and further enabled by the development of the Creative Commons licences. Lessig and others before him focus on the way traditional copyright law works against the development of mass intellectuality by restricting creativity and the collaborative, derivative development of knowledge. The dominant culture, he argues, is a 'permission culture', one in which 'creators get to create only with the permission of the powerful, or of creators from the past' (Lessig 2004: xiv).

Using rights guaranteed by copyright law, creative works produced under forms of this license can be distributed and modified by anyone, as long as the work remains attributable to the original authors (**creativecommons.org**). Dyer-Witheford (1999) refers to 'hackers', using the term in the original sense of someone who delights in a complete understanding of internal working of a computer system. These hackers have successfully employed similar 'open source' licenses for over twenty years (St. Laurent 2004) to protect both their work and its means of production. A Creative Commons license provides legal protection for copyright holders who wish to contribute to an open, social body of knowledge which transgresses the dominant operations of a capitalist economy by explicitly renouncing traditional intellectual property rights, and contributes to a mass intellect in commons. The Free Culture movement, based upon collaboratively producing intellectual and creative works under Creative Commons style licenses, therefore resists the restrictive control of traditional forms of legal protection designed to support the notion of 'intellectual property' and the 'permissive' economic model by which capital trades in such questionable assets (Lessig 2004). This enables both students and academics to do more than restructure curricula and pedagogy, but to challenge the very organizing principles upon which academic knowledge is currently being transmitted and produced. In this way, the student can truly be seen as a producer of knowledge.

Conclusion

In this chapter, we have set out to provide an overview of recent critical responses to the corporatization of higher education and the configuration of the student as consumer. We have also discussed the relationship between the core activities of teaching and research and reflected on both nineteenth century discourse and more recent efforts to re-establish the university as a liberal humanist institution, where teaching and research are equal and fundamental aspects of academic life. While recognizing recent efforts which acknowledge and go some way to addressing the need for enquiry-based learning and constructivist models of student participation, we have argued that a more critical approach is necessary to promote change at an institutional level. This critical approach looks at the wider social, political and economic context beyond the institution and introduces the work of Benjamin and other Marxist writers who have argued that a critique of the social relations of capitalist production is central to understanding and remodelling the role of the university and the relationship between academic and student.

The idea of student as producer encourages the development of collaborative relations between student and academic for the production of knowledge. However, if this idea is to connect to the project of refashioning in fundamental ways the nature of the university, then further attention needs to be paid to the framework by which the student as producer contributes towards mass intellectuality. This requires academics and students to do more than simply redesign their curricula, but go further and redesign the organizing principle, (i.e. private property and wage labour), through which academic knowledge is currently being produced. An exemplar alternative organizing principle is already proliferating in universities in the form of open, networked collaborative initiatives which are not intrinsically anti-capital but, fundamentally, ensure the free and creative use of research materials. Initiatives such as Science Commons, Open Knowledge and Open Access, are attempts by academics and others to lever the internet to ensure that research output is free to use, re-use and distribute without legal, social or technological restriction (**www.opendefinition.org**). Through these efforts, the organizing principle is being redressed creating a teaching, learning and research environment which promotes the values of openness and creativity, engenders equity among academics and students and thereby offers an opportunity to reconstruct the student as producer and academic as collaborator. In an environment where knowledge is free, the roles of the educator and the institution necessarily change. The educator is no longer a delivery vehicle and the institution becomes a landscape for the production and construction of a mass intellect in commons.

Conclusion – The Learning Landscape: Views with Endless Possibilities

11

Pam Locker

Introduction: navigating the learning landscape

The learning landscape is a restless place. Constantly shifting and resettling, erupting, changing, evolving. Its topography has undoubtedly been fundamentally shaped and reshaped by government, but its inhabitants continue to build on difficult terrain, supporting educational communities that are the foundations on which everything else relies.

So how can we successfully 'read' the learning landscape as it stands today and navigate our way safely towards the future? This collection of papers represents a series of thought-provoking markers that flag up possible changes in direction. Territory needs to be renegotiated, methods and approaches questioned, new tools and tactics applied and probably most problematic of all, the rethink of languages of learning brought about by technology needs to be accepted.

Our journey through the learning landscape begins with a reflection on the main policies that have shaped higher education as we recognize it today and a foundation against which to push for change, not just in the United Kingdom but in a global sense.

Stevenson and Bell in the Introduction discuss the idea of knowledge exchange transmitted through teaching and knowledge production focusing on producers generating new knowledge through research where there is systematic conversion of intellectual activity into intellectual capital and hence into intellectual property (Noble 1998). Knowledge has become a currency which generates a global knowledge economy and information society (Levidow 2002; Wright 2004) that is inevitably driven by the political aspirations of the governing power. According to Terence Karran in Chapter 2, the commercialization of higher education has created an accelerated system of producers and consumers who operate in a market-place of ideas in which knowledge is seen as a key human resource. For Karran, the quality of a country's education and research or knowledge production becomes a yardstick for its success within the global knowledge economy.

There is an imperative to recognize that change of policy is a never-ending journey whose direction will inevitably be dominated by government. From the relative autonomy of the 1950s Bell and Stevenson take us through a discourse via Bologna in 1988 and the dissolution of the polytechnics in the early nineties to Sir Ron Dearing's twenty-year vision of 1997 and the formation of the Higher Education Academy (NCIHE 1997). But Lord Leitch's report in 2006 delivers us to the consumer-driven higher education we recognize today. Only pragmatism and a positive approach to the possibilities of these evolutionary changes will enable us to see a way forward and continue to build on what exists with optimism.

Within a tight political context where political and academic interests may collide, Terence Karran in Chapter 2 discusses the ideal of academic freedom. He argues that levels of academic freedom reflect the academic and political health of a society and act as an indicator of our democratic freedoms. Academic freedom is implicit to the health of the nation as a questioning conscience; to lose it would threaten civilized society. It is a mechanism for a plurality of criticism that should be welcomed, bringing private corporations to account through expert criticism and through freedom of expression, encompassing a challenge to government.

While the nature of academic freedom as it exists in higher education is not without its critics, the benefits far outweigh the problems. Horwitz's view is that 'academic freedom is prized primarily because its contribution to truth seeking will yield discoveries or insights that ultimately will benefit society at large' (Horwitz 2005: 484).

Voices in the landscape

The government ambition that 50 per cent of school leavers should go on to higher education has not only resulted in management of increasing student numbers but has also meant a striking change in the student demographic. As Aileen Morris in Chapter 8 discusses, we face important issues about broadening access. Morris believes that for groups of students that are still underrepresented in universities 'that is, those defined as working class, disabled, from ethic minority groups' (Haselgrove 1994: 172), the university campus is an alien environment, which is unfamiliar and difficult to navigate. These students, even mature students studying at post-graduate level, often come feeling they are 'lacking in skills and culture' in an environment predominantly driven by the needs of young, middle class, digitally literate undergraduates. A change in approach is needed to create 'a new form of democratic learning' (Stuart 2000: 30) which encourages students to question the ownership of knowledge based on lived experience.

Andy Hagyard in Chapter 9 illustrates the growing importance of student surveys with the aim of ensuring that all members of the learning community have the opportunity to have a voice. In the United Kingdom for example, the National Student Survey cannot be ignored. As Sullivan (2007) claims, technology has made surveying much easier and few would deny the impact the Survey has had. Certainly as a national and local quality assurance mechanism it has raised the volume of the student voice and has compelled intuitions to review internal feedback and methodologies.

Although online surveys have been challenged for their lack of reliability they are now becoming more sophisticated, user friendly, and efficient. However there is a challenge that students suffer from survey fatigue, disillusioned and apathetic to poorly designed surveys. The challenge, then, is to create well designed material that students engage with. Hagyard argues that feedback needs to be 'systemic and cultural' and that the student community need to see that feedback is valued and acted upon. Consequently, feedback becomes part of the student's responsibility if they are to be valued members of the university community.

The voice of technology rings loud in the learning landscape. The idea of blended learning and its supporting technology has radically shifted from the first generation Web 1.0 based learning and is now challenged by the more socially interactive Web 2.0; there are murmurings of a semantic Web 3.0 (Anderson 2007). But many academics have been unable, or chosen not to respond to these changes. The evolving new technological landscape of higher education is one of 'digital natives and digital immigrants' (Prensky 2001). As academics we have the potential to become strangers in our own land. In Chapter 7, Sue Watling has identified this as a 'new digital divide' between our technologically literate students and academics who still prefer 'a pen over a keyboard'. New generations of students are 'wired differently' by their technologically-driven social and educational experiences, and arrive on campus with access to 'multiple learning landscapes'. It is inevitable that this has caused pedagogical tensions within the academic community; however if the pedagogic potential of technology is to be explored there is an urgent need to recognize and address these shortfalls in digital literacy, particularly as it is more often the educators who are the digital immigrants. On an even simpler level, what voices will be used and what languages learned to teach successfully?

The use of language should never be seen as a solely local concern. The development of technology has changed how we communicate globally, making world issues matters of local importance. Terfot Ngwana in Chapter 4 argues that for higher education this has meant that the nature of courses and curricula cannot be divorced from fundamental global issues. For environmentalists, issues of sustainability and sustainable development need be woven into the learning landscape of higher education. This must be done through appropriate programmes and pedagogy which will challenge the dissonance that often surrounds this issue and will also facilitate an understanding of sustainability literacy.

Supporting structures

Since 'staff expertise is the most important asset in a university; without it literally nothing can be achieved' (Blackmore and Blackwell 2003: 23), Continuing Professional Development (CPD) for staff is a key supporting structure within the learning landscape. But as Karin Crawford explains in Chapter 6, this process is not without tensions. As well as unclear definitions of the kind of activity that constitutes CPD, the uneasy relationships between policy, implementation, institutional and individual interests are for some seen negatively as a potentially disciplinary tool. While CPD is perceived by academics themselves as individual development, the implications of the *UK Professional Standards Framework for teaching and supporting learning in higher education*, (Higher Education Academy 2006) raise questions about whose needs are actually being met – those of the individual or those of the institution. While research is ongoing there appears to be a need for a more holistic approach to CPD, whereby institutions take responsibility for establishing CPD for staff within existing systems.

Of similar importance is the role of the Educational Development Unit (EDU), which plays a critical role in supporting change and enhancing teaching. Julian Beckton in Chapter 5 explores the role of EDUs in quality assurance and quality enhancement in the changing learning landscape of universities.

He argues that EDUs have tended to focus on technical enhancement for teaching and learning such as training staff to handle new technologies, for example the VLE. However this is often reactive and piecemeal rather than grounded in a clear conceptualization of good teaching and learning practices. Beckton recognizes the importance for further international research to explore of how teaching and learning materials can be shared and appropriate functions for EDUs in educational development established.

Evolving ecosystems

In recent years market forces and political restructuring have divided the academic community. There are 'two academic tribes – those who prioritize research and those who tend to prioritize teaching' (Ramsden, cited in Trigwell and Shale 2004: 523). A recurring theme in this book is the need for academics in higher education to renegotiate relationships, not only with each other but with their students. The call is for more democratic and interactive learning relationships where the passive learning of the past is replaced with active student researchers who play their part as knowledge producers.

Mike Neary and Joss Winn in Chapter 10 ask us to reconsider how we teach, learn and research and in doing so to question the core activity and purpose of the university. Neary and Winn highlight Boyer's four categories of scholarship which in essence produce an 'academic bill of rights'. Here there are opportunities to learn through enquiry rather than simply through the transmission of knowledge (Boyer Commission 1999). The reinvention of students as student producers would require engagement in problem- and enquiry-based learning and form the basis of their student experience. Exciting educational experiments at Centres for Excellence in Teaching and Learning (CETLs) such as Sheffield University's 'Collaboratory' and Warwick University's 'Reinvention Centre' are examples of how students can make this transition to take a more interactive role in their learning.

Places for learning and spaces that learn

Running parallel with the debate about nature and role of the university is a discourse that questions preconceived ideas about physical teaching spaces in the learning landscape. How do campus spaces need to be redesigned or adapted to accommodate new approaches to teaching, learning and research?

While technology has revolutionized the way we live globally, the vast majority of our higher education spaces appear unchanged. Wireless technology facilitates mobile learning that can take place anywhere and students are taking advantage of this by colonising and creating their own social learning spaces. Lefebvre's ideas (1991) about not shutting down possibilities for space through permanency echo what is happening in reality. But for educators there needs to be a constructed alignment between curriculum and space. The politics of space begs questions of control. Is the use of space driven by pedagogy or curricular demands? (Barnett 2007: 4). In pedagogical spaces, 'students can become authentically themselves' (Barnett 2007: 141). Mike Neary and Angela Thody in Chapter 3 talk about the need for a relationship between pedagogy and design in architecture, to demonstrate a clear pedagogic rationale for decisions. Too often decisions are opportunistic but education needs intelligent spaces that can support a variety of types of learning, including the virtual. The involvement of pedagogic theory and the joining of the academic voice to the architectural provide an intellectual and critical dimension to the spaces themselves, suggesting further possibilities for how the spaces might be developed, in a process that Lefebvre refers to as 'ideas of endless possibilities'.

Conclusion: the views with endless possibilities

The learning landscape has a complicated, delicately balanced and continually evolving ecosystem. As Charles Darwin is reputed to have said by Hamp (2007) among others, 'it is not the strongest of the species that survives, nor the most intelligent, but the one most responsive to change'.

The first decade of the twenty-first century has heralded unprecedented change in higher education and this series of papers reflects much of this change. There are four overarching themes that appear key in the future development of the learning landscape:

- a call for Democracy;
- the need for Technology;

- the value of Pedagogy;
- how to navigate Policy.

'A new form of democracy' (Stuart 2000: 30) requires the courage to renegotiate institutional relationships in order to find 'a more democratic dialogue between academics and students' (Thompson 2000: 10). The elite systems of the past have been broken down as mass higher education becomes established, but this brings with it new challenges and pressures for the stretched academy. This new democracy needs to be accessible and all inclusive.

Technology has the potential to be a great democratizing influence, particularly the internet as a 'quintessential intuition of general intellect' (Dyer-Witheford 1999: 498). Digital learners of the future are more likely to speak as one voice through social and other collaborative networks and Marx's definition for mass education rings true here: 'polycentric, communicatively-connected, collective intelligence' (Dyer-Witheford 1999: 498). Technology is also a potentially powerful political tool for students and institutions, as exemplified by the experience of student surveys.

A truce is required for old tribal wars between researchers and teachers, which are divisive in the learning landscape. Instead, new alliances between research-driven academics and students reinvented as producers signal exciting collaborative opportunities to generate new knowledge. A democracy of space will bring with it endless possibilities as a wirelessly-connected, mobile student body reclaims places and spaces between places as their own. It will not only be challenging to design new intelligent educational environments but also to reinvent existing teaching and learning spaces as relevant flexible spaces for twenty-first century learning. This may even require a new area of educational design with a sound understanding of 'sustainability literacy'. Ultimately, as Crawford argues in Chapter 6, the quality and effectiveness of work place environments can be seen as a central means of creating cultures of concern for enhancing teaching and learning.

Effective and sustainable evolution for higher education will require a pedagogical quest through the learning landscape. Whether in relation to professional development, the reinvention of educational spaces, the application of technology, the alignment of curriculum or our relationship with research, as new ideas emerge we need to build a theoretical framework for support. The underpinning of this infrastructure needs to be via pedagogic critique. In essence the cumulative effect of this will be to question the very nature of the university and its role in twenty-first century education. What is teaching? What is learning? Indeed, what is pedagogy? We need a much clearer understanding of the changing student demographic. The challenges are not simply about managing large numbers, but questioning our understanding of a different type of student population with unfamiliar needs.

The onslaught of technology and the 'clicker' generation has found some of us out of sync with our students. Is it acceptable for academics to be digitally illiterate if we are to have any chance of bridging the digital divide? This will not be an easy transition and a pragmatic two-way traffic approach allowing both the analogue and digital will be required. However, issues of both staff and student digital illiteracy may exacerbate as technology burgeons on and the role of EDUs, CPD and other institutional and personal support systems become ever more imperative.

The increasing mobility of learning can take place virtually anywhere and anywhere provides opportunities to learn virtually. It is most likely that students themselves will drive the use of technology in the future, but it is essential that institutions are forward thinking in order for infrastructures to be flexible enough to support change. If we are to build communities that can effectively communicate, it is also important that human needs run alongside technological developments. It would be easy following the very public collapse of the e-university to underestimate the potential of e-learning. But one is reminded of Isambard Kingdom Brunel's wide gauge Great Western Railway. The width of the rail may have been wrong, but the railway was here to stay!

In all areas of higher education from management and communication systems to feedback, social networking exploiting Web 2.0 and 3.0, the 'disruptive technology of internet has been a powerful agent for change' (Anderson and Elloumi 2004: xv). In the learning landscape of the future, engagement with technology has the potential to become a matter of survival or extinction. Encompassing all of this, we have to acknowledge the influence and power of the political landscape both at national and institutional levels. We will need to find ways to navigate our way confidently onwards through the unavoidable pressures of public accountability and league tables, but must not be distracted from the importance of what we do as educators. Technology is helping to inform as well as question the political process. Market economics have transformed knowledge into a global currency, but we need to find ways to challenge the assumptions of the neo-liberal university. In conclusion, what challenges lie ahead of us in an uncharted learning landscape? This collection of papers has thrown up more questions then answers. Can we hope for a time when the landscape will level and settle? Probably not. But with optimism and a spirit of exploration it could be an exciting journey. The future is waiting for our influence. All we can do is take the first unsure steps and believe in a land full of endless possibilities.

References

Adomssent, M., Godemann, J. and Michelsen, G. (2007), 'Transferability of approaches to sustainable development at universities as a challenge', *International Journal of Sustainability in Higher Education*, 8, (4), 385–402.

Adorno, T. W. (1966), *Negative Dialectics* trans. E. B. Ashton (1973). New York: Seabury Press.

Aldrich, C. T. (2006), 'E-Learning in the workplace', *Training and Development*, 60, (9), 54–60.

Allan, C., Blackwell, R. and Gibbs, G. (2003), 'Developing the subject dimension to staff development', in R. Blackwell and P. Blackmore (eds), *Towards Strategic Staff Development in Higher Education*. Berkshire: Open University, pp. 66–78.

Allen, M. (1988), *The Goals of Universities*. Buckingham: SRHE/Open University Press.

Anderson, P. (2007), 'What is Web 2.0? Ideas, technologies and implications for education', *JISC Technology and Standards Watch*, [online] www.jisc.ac.uk/media/documents/techwatch/tsw0701b.pdf.

Anderson, T. and Elloumi, F. (2004), 'Introduction', in T. Anderson and F. Elloumi (eds), *Theory and Practice of Online Learning*. Canada: Athabasca University, pp. xiii–xxiv.

Arthur, M. and Lindsay, V. J. (2006), *Knowledge at Work: Creative Collaboration in the Global Economy*. London: Blackwell.

Atherton, J. S. (2005), *Learning and Teaching: Cognitive Dissonance and Learning*. [online] www.learningandteaching.info/learning/dissonance.htm.

Attali, J. (1998), *Pour un Modèle Européen d'Enseignement Supérieur*. Paris: Ministère de l'Éducation Nationale, de la Recherche et de la Technologie.

Attwood, R. (2008), 'Probe ordered into "manipulation" ', *Times Higher Education Supplement*, 28 February.

Bamber, J., Ducklin, A. and Tett, L. (2000), 'Working with contradictions in the struggle for access', in J. Thompson (ed.), *Stretching the Academy*. Leicester: NIACE, pp. 158–70.

Barnett, R. (2000), *Realising the University in an Age of Supercomplexity*. Buckingham: Society for Research into Higher Education with Open University Press.

Barnett, R. (2005a), 'Introduction', in R. Barnett (ed.) *Reshaping the University: New Relationships between Research, Scholarship and Teaching*. Maidenhead: Society for Research into Higher Education and Open University Press, pp. 1–8.

Barnett, R. (2005b), 'Recapturing the universal in the university', *Educational Philosophy and Theory*, 37, (6), 785–97.

Barnett, R. (ed.) (2005c), *Reshaping the University: New Relationships between Research, Scholarship and Teaching*. Berkshire: Open University Press.

Barnett, R. (2007), *A Will To Learn: Being a Student in an Age of Uncertainty*. Maidenhead and New York: Society for Research into Higher Education.

Barnett, R. and Temple, P. (2006), *Impact on Space of Future Changes in Higher Education* (UK Higher Education Space Management Project, 2006–2010). Bristol: Higher Education Funding Council for England.

Barr, R. and Tagg, J. (1995), 'From teaching to learning: a new paradigm for undergraduate education', [online] **critical.tamucc.edu/~blalock/readings/tch2learn.htm**.

Barth, M., Godemann, J., Riechmann, M. and Stoltenberg, U. (2007), 'Developing key competencies for sustainable development in higher education', *International Journal of Sustainable Development in Higher Education*, 8, (4), 416–30.

Becher, T. and Kogan, M. (1983), 'A model for higher education', in O. Boyd-Barrett, T. Bush, J. Goodey, I. McNay and M. Preedy (eds), *Approaches to Post-School Management*. London: Harper and Row, pp. 14–28.

Becher, T. and Trowler, P. (2001), *Academic Tribes and Territories: Intellectual Enquiry and the Culture of Disciplines*. Buckingham: SRHE with Open University Press.

Beckerman, W. (1994), 'Sustainable development: is it a useful concept?', *Environmental Values*, 3, (3), 191–209.

Bell, D. (1973), *The Coming of the Post-Industrial Society*. New York: Basic Books.

Bell, L. (2007), *Perspectives on Educational Management and Leadership*. London: Continuum Books.

Bell, L. and Stevenson, H. (2006), *Education Policy: Process, Themes and Impact*. London: Routledge.

Bell, M. and Bell, W. (2005), 'It's installed . . . now get on with it! Looking beyond the software to the cultural change', *British Journal of Educational Technology*, 36, (4), 643–56.

Beloff, M. (1968), *The Plate Glass Universities*. London: Secker and Warburg.

Benjamin, W. (1915), 'The life of students', in M. Bullock and M. W. Jennings (eds) (2004), *Walter Benjamin: Selected Writings, Volume 1, 1913–1926*. Harvard: Harvard University Press, pp. 37–47.

Benjamin, W. (1934), 'The author as producer', in M. W. Jennings, H. Eiland and G. Smith (eds) (2005), *Walter Benjamin: Selected Writings, Volume 2, 1927–1934*. Harvard: Harvard University Press, pp. 768–82.

Bergan, S. (2003), 'Institutional autonomy between myth and responsibility', in *Autonomy and Responsibility: The University's Obligations for the XXIst Century*. Bologna: Bononia University Press, pp. 49–67.

Berners-Lee, T. (1997), 'Realising the full potential of the Web', [online] www.w3.org/1998/02/Potential.html

Biggs, J. (2003), *Teaching for Quality Learning at University: What the Student Does*. Maidenhead: Society for Research into Higher Education and Open University Press.

Billett, S. R. (2002), 'Critiquing workplace learning discourses: participation and continuity at work', *Studies in the Education of Adults*, 34, (1), 56–67.

Blackmore, P. and Blackwell, R. (2003), 'Academic roles and relationships' in R. Blackwell and P. Blackmore (eds), *Towards Strategic Staff Development in Higher Education*. Berkshire: Open University Press, pp. 16–28.

Blackmore, P. and Blackwell, R. (2006), 'Strategic leadership in academic development', *Studies in Higher Education*, 31, (3), 373–87.

Blackwell, R. and Blackmore, P. (eds) (2003a), *Towards Strategic Staff Development in Higher Education*. Berkshire: Open University Press.

Blackwell, R. and Blackmore, P. (2003b), 'Rethinking strategic staff development', in R. Blackwell and P. Blackmore (eds), *Towards Strategic Staff Development in Higher Education*. Berkshire: Open University Press, pp. 3–15.

Bligh, D. (1972), *What's the Use of Lectures?* Harmondsworth: Penguin.

Bloom, B. S. and Krathwol, D. R. (1956), *Taxonomy of Educational Objectives: The Classification of Educational Goals*. New York: David McKay Company, Inc.

Boden, R. and Epstein, D. (2006), 'Managing the research imagination? Globalisation and research in higher education', *Globalisation, Societies and Education*, 4, (2), 223–36.

Bohner, G. and Wänke M. (2002), *Attitudes and Attitude Change*. Sussex: Psychology Press.

Bonefeld, W. (1995), 'The politics of debt: social discipline and control', *Common Sense*, 17, June, [online] www.wildcat-www.de/en/material/cs17bone.htm

Bourgeois, E. and Frenay, M. (2001), University Adult Access Policies and Practices across the European Union, and their Consequences for the Participation of Non-Traditional Adults. Final Report to the European Commission of TSER Project SOE2-CT97–2021.

Bowl, M. (2003*), Non-traditional Entrants to Higher Education: 'They Talk About People Like Me'*. Stoke on Trent: Trentham.

Boyer, E. (1990), *Scholarship Reconsidered: Priorities for the Professoriate*. Princeton, NJ: Carnegie Foundation for the Advancement of Teaching.

Boyer Commission (1999), *Reinventing Undergraduate Education: A Blueprint for America's Research Universities*. Stony Brook, NY: Carnegie Foundation for University Teaching.

Brady, T., Marchall, N., Prencipe, A. and Tell, F. (2002), 'Making sense of learning landscapes in project-based organisations', paper presented at the Third European Conference on Organizational Knowledge, Learning and Capabilities, Athens, Greece, 5–6 April.

Brennan, J. and Jary, D. (2005), What is Learned at University? SOMUL Working Paper 1, York: Higher Education Academy.

Brennan, J. and Osborne, M. (2005), The Organisational Mediation of University Learning. SOMUL Working Paper 2, York: Higher Education Academy.

Brennan, J. and Williams, R. (2004), Collecting and using student feedback, a guide to good practice. CHERI [online] www.heacademy.ac.uk/resources/detail/Collecting_and_using_student_feedback.

Brew, A. (2006), *Research and Teaching: Beyond the Divide*. Basingstoke: Palgrave Macmillan.

Bricall, J. M. (2000), *Universidad Dos Mil* ('Informe Bricall'). Madrid: CRUE.

Broers, A. (2005), 'University courses for tomorrow' the third annual Higher Education Policy Institute lecture, Royal Institution, London, 24 November, [online] www.hepi.ac.uk/pubdetail.asp?ID=188&DOC=Lectures.

Brown, J. S. and Duguid, P. (1995), 'The university in the digital age', [online] www.johnseely-brown.com/DigitalU.pdf.

Bruner, J. (1986), *Actual Minds, Possible Worlds*. Cambridge, MA: Harvard University Press.

Buchan, G. D., Spellerberg, I. F. and Blum, W. E. H. (2007), 'Education for sustainability: developing a postgraduate-level subject with an international perspective', *International Journal for Sustainability in Higher Education*, 8, (1), 4–15.

Burgess, T. (1979), 'New ways to Learn'. *Journal of the Royal Society of Arts*, 128, 143–55.

Bush, V. (1945), *Science: The Endless Frontier*. Washington: United States Government Printing Office.

Calder, W. and Clugston, R. M. (2003), 'Progress toward sustainability in higher education', *Environmental Law Reporter*, 33, 1003–23.

Carroll, J. and Appleton, J. (2001), Plagiarism: A good practice guide. [online] www.jisc.ac.uk/uploaded_documents/brookes.pdf.

Castells, M. (2000), *The Rise of the Network Society*. Oxford: Blackwell.

Chiddick, D. (2006), 'Performing in a blend of real and virtual worlds', in DEGW, Working to learn, learning to work: Design in educational transformation, 4th Annual Foundation Lecture, pp. 22–4.

Chiddick, D. (2007), 'Learning landscapes', unpublished lecture, Senior Management Group, University of Lincoln.

CIBER (2008), Information behaviour of the student of the future. CIBER Briefing Paper. [online] www.ucl.ac.uk/slais/research/ciber/downloads/.

Claxton, G. (1994), 'Involuntary simplicity: changing dysfunctional habits of consumption', *Environmental Values*, 3, 71–8.

Clegg, S. (2003a), 'Learning and teaching policies in higher education: mediations and contradictions of practice', *British Educational Research Journal*, 29, (6), 803–19.

Clegg, S. (2003b), 'Problematising ourselves: Continuing Professional Development in higher education', *International Journal for Academic Development*, 8, (1/2), 37–50.

Clugston, R. M. and Calder, W. (1999), 'Critical dimensions of sustainability in higher education', in W. Leal Filho (ed.), *Sustainability and University Life*. Frankfurt: Peter Lang, pp. 31–46.

Cole, M. (1990), 'Cognitive development and formal schooling; the evidence from cross-cultural research', in L. Moll (ed.), *Vygotsky and Education: Instructional Implications and Applications of Sociohistorical Psychology*. Cambridge: Cambridge University Press, pp. 89–110.

Collier, K. (1982), 'Ideological influences in higher education', in *Studies in Higher Education*, 7, (1), 13–19.

Collis, B. (1999), 'Telematics-supported education for traditional universities in Europe', *Performance Improvement Quarterly*, 12, (2), 36–65.

Colucci-Gray, L. (2006), 'From scientific literacy to sustainability literacy: an ecological framework for education', *Science Education*, 90, (2), 227–52.

Committee on Higher Education (1963), Higher Education Report of the Committee appointed by the Prime Minister under the Chairmanship of Lord Robbins 1961–1963 (The Robbins Report). London: HMSO Cmnd 2154.

Conole, G., de Laat, M., Dillon, T. and Darby, J. (2006), LXP: Student experiences of technologies. Final report. [online] www.jisc.ac.uk/media/documents/programmes/elearning_pedagogy/lxp%20project%20final%20report%20dec%2006.pdf.

Cortese, A. (1999), *Education for Sustainable Development: The Need for a New Human Perspective*. Boston, MA: Second Nature.

Cotton, D. R. E., Warren, M. F., Maiboroda, O. and Bailey, I. (2007), 'Sustainable development, higher education and pedagogy: a study of lecturers' beliefs and attitudes', *Journal of Environmental Education Research*, 13, (5), 579–97.

Creanor, L., Trinder, K., Gowan, D. and Howells, C. (2006), LEX: The learner experience of e-Learning. Final report. [online] www.jisc.ac.uk/uploaded_documents/LEX%20Final%20Report_August06.pdf

Crowther, J., Martin, I. and Shaw, M. (2000), 'Turning the discourse', in J. Thompson (ed.), *Stretching the Academy*. Leicester: NIACE, pp. 171–85.

CRQ (Centre for Research into Quality) (2006), Student satisfaction electronic pilot. [online] www0.bcu.ac.uk/crq/electronic.htm

Cullingford, C. (2002), 'Institutional development and professional needs: some reflections', in G. Trorey and C. Cullingford (eds), *Professional Development and Institutional Needs*. Aldershot: Ashgate Publishing, pp. 223–35.

Cutright, M. (ed.) (2001), *Chaos Theory and Higher Education: Leadership, Planning and Policy*. New York: Peter Lang.

D'Andrea, V. and Gosling, D. (2005), *Improving Teaching and Learning in Higher Education: A Whole Institution Approach*. Berkshire: Open University Press.

De Angelis, M. and Harvie, D. (2006), Cognitive capitalism and the rat race – how capitalism measures ideas and affects. [online] www.geocities.com/immateriallabour/angelisharviea-bstract2006.html

Dealty, R. (2002), 'The real-time corporate university becomes a reality', *Journal of Workplace Learning*, 14, (8), 340–8.

DEFRA (1999), *A Better Quality of Life – Strategy for Sustainable Development for the United Kingdom*. Department for Environment, Food and Rural Affairs, Cmnd 4345.

DEFRA (2005), *Securing the Future: Delivering UK Sustainable Development Strategy*. Department for Environment, Food and Rural Affairs, 6467.

DEGW (2006), 'Working to learn, learning to work: design in educational transformation', 4th Annual Foundation Lecture, DEGW, [online] www.DEGW.com.

DEGW (2007), Learning landscape. [online] www.buffalo.edu/ub2020/plan/files/forum1/Learning-Landscape.pdf

Dewey, J. (1963*), Experience in Education*. New York: MacMillan.

DfES (Department for Education and Skills) (2003), *The Future of Higher Education*. Norwich: The Stationery Office.

Dill, D. D. (2005), 'The degradation of the academic ethic: teaching, research and the renewal of professional self-regulation', in R. Barnett (ed.), *Reshaping the University*. Berkshire: Open University Press, pp. 178–91.

Domask, J. (2007), 'Achieving goals in higher education: an experiential approach to sustainability studies', *International Journal of Sustainability in Higher Education*, 8, (1), 53–68.

Downes, S. (2004), 'Educational blogging', *Educause Review*, 39, (5), 14–26. [online] www. educause.edu/pub/er/erm04/erm0450.asp?bhcp=1

Drucker, P. (1969), *The Age of Discontinuities*. London: Transaction Publications.

Dworkin R. (1996), 'Objectivity and truth: you'd better believe it', *Philosophy & Public Affairs*, 25, 87–139.

Dyer-Witheford, N. (1999), *Cyber-Marx: Cycles and Circuits of Struggle in High-Technology Capitalism*. Urbana and Chicago: University of Illinois Press.

Edwards, B. (2000), *University Architecture*. London: Spon Press.

Edwards, R. and Usher, R. (eds) (2003), *Space, Curriculum and Learning*. Greenwich, CT: IAP.

Elton, L. (1994), *Management of Teaching and Learning: Towards Change in Universities*. London: CVCP/SRHE.

Enders, J. and de Weert, E. (2004), *The International Attractiveness of the Academic Workplace in Europe*. Frankfurt/Main: Gewerkschaft Erziehung und Wissenschaft.

Erwin, P. (2001), *Attitudes and Persuasion*. Sussex: Psychology Press.

ETL (2000/2001), Enhancing teaching-learning environments in undergraduate courses (Project Proposal to ESRC). University of Edinburgh. [online] www.ed.ac.uk/etl

ETL (2002), ETL Project Progress Report. [online] www.ed.ac.uk/etl

ETL (2003), ETL Project Progress Report. [online] www.ed.ac.uk/etl

ETL (2004), ETL Project Progress Report. [online] www.ed.ac.uk/etl

ETL (2005), ETL Project Progress Report. [online] www.ed.ac.uk/etl

EUA (European Universities Association), (1988), *Magna Charta Universitatum*. Bologna: EUA.

Evans, M. (2004), *Killing Thinking: The Death of the Universities*. London and New York: Continuum Press.

Farrell, H. (2005), 'The blogosphere as a carnival of ideas', *Chronicle of Higher Education*, [online] chronicle.com/free/v52/i07/07b01401.htm

Fearn, H. (2008), 'Clocking on', *Times Higher Education Supplement*, 1 May.

Field, J. (2002), 'Governing the ungovernable: why lifelong learning policies promise so much yet deliver so little', in R. Edwards, N. Miller, N. Small and A. Tait (eds), *Supporting Lifelong Learning* Volume 3, Making Policy Work. London: Routledge, pp. 201–16.

Fisch, K. (2007), 'Is it okay to be a technologically illiterate teacher?', [online] thefischbowl. blogspot.com/2007/09/is-it-okay-to-be-technologically.html

Flint, R. W., McCarter, W. and Bonniwell, W. M. A. T. (2000), 'Interdisciplinary education in sustainability: links in secondary and higher education. The Northampton Legacy Program', *International Journal of Sustainability in Higher Education*, 1, (2), 191–202.

Forsyth, A. and Furlong, A. (2000), *Socioeconomic Disadvantage and Access to Higher Education*. Bristol: Policy Press.

Foucault, M. (2005), *History of Madness*, trans. J. Murphy and J. Khalfa. London: Routledge.

Fowler, G. (1983), 'Past failure and the imperative for change', in O. Boyd-Barrett, T. Bush, J. Goodey, I. McNay and M. Preedy (eds), *Approaches to Post-School Management*. London: Harper and Row, pp. 119–32.

Francis, R. and Raftery, J. (2005), 'Blended learning landscapes', *Brookes eJournal of Learning and Teaching*, 1, (3), 1–5, [online] **bejlt.brookes.ac.uk**

Freire, P. (1970), *Pedagogy of the Oppressed*. London: Penguin.

Fuller, S. (2005), *The Intellectual: The Positive Power of Negative*. Cambridge: Icon Books.

Garrison, D. R. and Anderson, T. (2003), *E-learning in the 21st Century: A Framework for Research and Practice*. London: Routledge Falmer.

Gibbs, P., Angelides, P. and Michaelides, P. (2004), 'Preliminary thoughts on a praxis of higher education teaching', *Teaching in Higher Education*, 9, (2), 183–94.

Giddens, A. (1981), *A Contemporary Critique of Historical Materialism*. London: Macmillan.

Gilbert, A. D. (2000), 'The idea of a university beyond 2000', *Policy*, St Leonard's Centre for Independent Policy Studies in Australia and New Zealand, 16, (1), 31–6.

Giles, J. (2005), 'internet encyclopaedias go head to head', *Nature*, 438, 900–01, 15 December, [online] www.nature.com/nature/journal/v438/n7070/full/438900a.html

Goldstein, S. R. (1976), 'The asserted constitutional right of public school teachers to determine what they teach', *University of Pennsylvania Law Review*, 124, 1293–357.

Gombrich, R. (2000), 'British higher education in the last twenty years: the murder of a profession', lecture given to the Graduate Institute of Policy Studies, Tokyo, 7 January.

Gorard, S., Smith, E., May, H., Thomas, L., Admett, N. and Slack, K. (2006), Review of widening participation research: addressing the barriers to participation in higher education, report to HEFCE by the University of York, Higher Education Academy and Institute for Access Studies.

Gosling, D. (2001), 'Educational Development Units in the UK – what are they doing five years on', *International Journal for Academic Development*, 6, (1), 74–89.

Gosling, D. (2008), *Educational Development in the United Kingdom*. London: Heads of Educational Development Group. http://www.hedg.ac.uk/documents/HEDG_Report_final.pdf

Guile, D. (2006), 'What is distinctive about the knowledge economy? Implications for education', in H. Lauder, P. Brown, J. Dillabough and A. H. Halsey (eds), *Education, Globalization and Social Change*. Oxford: Oxford University Press, pp. 355–66.

Haggis, T. (2006), 'Pedagogies for diversity: retaining critical challenge amidst fears of "dumbing down" ', *Studies in Higher Education*, 31, (5), 521–35.

Hamp, I. (2007), Survival of the most adaptable. [online] www.iainhamp.com/goals/2007/09/22/survival-of-the-most-adaptable

Hanson, A. (1996), 'The search for a separate theory of adult learning: does anyone really need andragogy?', in R. Edwards, A. Hanson and P. Raggatt (eds), *Boundaries of Adult Learning*. London: Routledge, cited in H. Peters, H. Pokorny, and A. Sheibani, (1999), 'Fitting in: what place is accorded to the experiential learning mature students bring with them to higher education', paper presented to SCUTREA, 29th Annual Conference, University of Warwick, 6 July.

Hardt, M. and Negri, A. (2000), *Empire*. Cambridge: Harvard University Press.

Hartman, J., Moskal, P. and Dziuban, C. (2005), 'Preparing the academy of today for the learner of tomorrow', in D. G. Oblinger and J. L. Oblinger (eds), *Educating the Net Generation*. EDUCAUSE E-Book [online] www.educause.edu/IsItAgeorIT%3AFirstStepsTowardUnderstandingtheNetGeneration/6062

Harvey, D. (2000), *Spaces of Hope*. Edinburgh: Edinburgh University Press.

Harvey, L. (2003a), 'Scrap that student survey now', *Times Higher Education Supplement*, 12 December.

Harvey, L. (2003b), 'Student feedback', *Quality in Higher Education*, 9, (1), 3–20.

Haselgrove, S. (ed.) (1994), *The Student Experience*. Buckingham: SRHE and Open University Press.

Haskell, T. (1996), 'Justifying the right of academic freedom in the era of "power/knowledge" ', in L. Menand (ed.), *The Future of Academic Freedom*. Chicago: University of Chicago Press, pp. 43–92.

Hattie, J. and Marsh, H. W. (1996), 'The relationship between research and teaching: a meta-analysis', *Review of Educational Research*, 66, (4), 507–42.

HEA (Higher Education Academy) (2006), The UK Professional Standards Framework for teaching and supporting learning in higher education. [online] www.heacademy.ac.uk

HEA (Higher Education Academy) (2007), 'Comparative review of British, American and Australian national surveys of undergraduate students', [online] www.heacademy.ac.uk/resources/detail/ourwork/research/NSS_comparative_review_resource.

Healey, M., Jordan, F., Barney, P. and Short, C. (forthcoming) The Research-Teaching Nexus: Student Experiences of Research and Consultancy, *Innovations in Education and Teaching International*.

HEFCE (Higher Education Funding Council for England) (2001), Quality Assurance in Higher Education. [online] www.hefce.ac.uk/pubs/hefce/2001/01_45.htm

HEFCE (Higher Education Funding Council for England) (2002a), Partnerships for Progression: Circular 2002/49. Bristol: HEFCE.

HEFCE (Higher Education Funding Council for England) (2002b), Information on Quality and Standards in Higher Education: Final report of the task group (The Cooke Report). [online] www.hefce.ac.uk/pubs/hefce/2002/02_15.htm

HEFCE (Higher Education Funding Council for England) (2005), HEFCE strategy for elearning. [online] www.hefce.ac.uk/pubs/hefce/2005/05_12/

Helmholtz, H. von (1877), 'On academic freedom in German universities', reprinted in D. Cahan (1995) (ed.), *Science & Culture: Popular & Philosophical Lectures*. Chicago: University of Chicago Press, pp. 328–41.

Hendley, B. (2002), 'Hofstetter, the romantic idea of a university', *History of Education Quarterly*, 42, (3), 418–20.

HEPS (Higher Education Partnership for Sustainability) (2003), *Reporting for Sustainability: Guidance for Higher Education Institutions*. London: Forum for the Future.

Hernes, G. (1993), 'Images of institutions of higher education', *Higher Education Management*, 5, 265–71.

Hockings, C., Cooke, S. and Bowl, M. (2007), ' "Academic engagement" within a widening participation context – a 3D analysis', *Teaching in Higher Education*, 12 (5/6), 721–33.

Hofstadter, R. and Metzger, W. (1955), *The Development of Academic Freedom in the United States*. New York: Columbia University Press.

Holland, S. (2003), *Council for College and University English News*, 17, Spring 2003. [online] www.ccue.ac.uk/fileadmin/documents/0208_CCUE_NEWS_MAR_APR.PDF

hooks, b. (1984), *Feminist Theory: From Margin to Centre*. Boston, MA: South End Press.

hooks, b. (1990), *Yearning: Race, Gender and Cultural Politics*. Toronto: Between the Lines Press.

Horwitz, P. (2005), 'Grutter's first amendment', *Boston College Law Review*, 46, (3), 461–590.

House of Commons (2005), UK e–University. House of Commons Education and Skills Committee, London: The Stationery Office.

Hubbard, P., Kitchin, R. and Valentine, G. (2007), *Key Thinkers on Space and Place*. Sage: London.

Humboldt, W. von (1810), 'On the spirit and organisational framework of intellectual institutions in Berlin', reprinted 1970, *Minerva*, 8, 242–67.

Hutchinson, D. (2004), *A Natural History of Place in Education*. New York: Teachers' College Press.

James, P. and Hopkinson, P. (2004), Sustainable Buildings Can Benefit Higher Education. A Briefing Paper, Higher Education Environmental Performance Improvement Project (HEEPI).

Jamieson, P. (2003), 'Designing more effective on-campus teaching and learning spaces: a role for academic developers', *International Journal for Academic Development*, 8, 119–33.

JISC (2003–2007), e-Learning Pedagogy Programme. [online] www.jisc.ac.uk/whatwedo/programmes/elearning_pedagogy.

JISC (2007), In their own words: exploring the learner's perspective on e-learning. [online] www.jiscinfonet.ac.uk/publications/in-their-own-words.

Kagawa, F. (2007), 'Dissonance in students' perception of sustainable development and sustainability: implications for curriculum change', *International Journal for Sustainability in Higher Education*, 8, (3), 317–38.

Kamradt, T. F. and Kamradt, E. J. (1999), 'Structured design for attitudinal instruction', in C. M. Reigeluth (ed.), *Instructional-Design Theories and Models*. London: Lawrence Erlbaum Associates, pp. 563–90.

Kerr, C. (1963), *The Uses of the University*. Cambridge: Harvard University Press.

Kerr, I. (1999), 'Newman's idea of an university', *Higher Education Policy Series*, 51, 11–29.

Keyishian v. Board of Regents of the State Univ. of New York (1967), 385 U.S. 589 603.

Knight, P. (2006), 'Quality enhancement and educational professional development', *Quality in Higher Education*, 12, (1), 29–40.

Knight, P. T. (2002), *Being a Teacher in Higher Education*. Buckingham: SRHE and Open University Press.

Knight, P. T. and Trowler, P. R. (2001), *Departmental Leadership in Higher Education*. Buckingham: Society for Research into Higher Education and Open University Press, cited in

S. Clegg, (2003), 'Problematising ourselves: Continuing Professional Development in higher education', *International Journal for Academic Development*, 8, (1/2), 37–50.

Knoll, J. H. and Siebert, H. (1967), *Humboldt: Politician and Educationalist*. Inter Nationes: Bad Godesberg.

Knowles, M. (1984), *The Adult Learner, a Neglected Species* (3rd edn). Houston: Gulf Publishing Company.

Kogan, M. (1975), *Educational Policy-Making: A Study of Interest Groups and Parliament*. London: George Allen and Unwin Ltd.

Kuhn, T. (1970), *The Structure of Scientific Revolutions*. Chicago: Chicago University Press.

Kwon, M. P. (2004), *One Place after Another: Site Specific Art and Location Identity*. Cambridge, MA: MIT Press.

Lamb, B. (2004), 'Wide open space: wikis, ready or not', *Educause Review*, 39, (5), 36–48, [online] www.educause.edu/pub/er/erm04/erm0452.asp

Lambert, C. (2008), 'Exploring new learning and teaching spaces', *Warwick Interactions Journal*, 11, (2), [online] www2.warwick.ac.uk/services/ldc/resource/interactions/current/ablambert

Lammers, W. and Murphy, J. (2002), 'A profile of teaching techniques used in the university classroom', *Active Learning in Higher Education*, 3, (1), 54–67.

Land, R. (2001), 'Agency, context and change in academic development', *Higher Education Quarterly*, 54, 207–16, cited in S. Clegg, (2003), 'Problematising ourselves: Continuing Professional Development in higher education', *International Journal for Academic Development*, 8, (1/2), 37–50.

Lauder, H., Brown, P., Dillabough, J. and Halsey, A. H. (2006), 'Introduction: the prospects for education: individualization, globalization and social change', in H. Lauder, P. Brown, J. Dillabough and A. H. Halsey (eds), *Education, Globalization and Social Change*. Oxford: Oxford University Press, pp. 1–70.

Laurillard, D. (2002), *Rethinking University Teaching: A Conversational Framework for the Effective Use of Learning Technologies* (2nd edn). London: RoutledgeFalmer.

Leathwood, C. (2001), 'The road to independence? Policy, pedagogy and the independent learner in higher education', in L. West, N. Miller, D. O'Reilly and R. Allen (eds), Proceedings of the 31st Annual Conference of SCUTREA, Pilgrim College, University of Nottingham: Nottingham, cited in B. Read, L. Archer and C. Leathwood (2003), 'Challenging cultures? Student conceptions of 'belonging' and 'isolation' at a post 1992 university', *Studies in Higher Education*, 28, (3), 261–77.

Lefebvre, H. (1991), *The Production of Space*. Oxford: Blackwell Publishing.

Leitch, S. (2006), *Prosperity for All in the Global Economy: World Class Skills: Final Report*. London: The Stationery Office.

Lenhart, A., Horrigan, J., Rainie, A., Boyce, A., Madden, M. and O'Grady, E. (2002), 'The ever-shifting internet population: a new look at internet access and the digital divide', *PEW Internet and American Life Project*, [online] www.pewinternet.org/report_display.asp?r=88

Lessig, L. (2004), *Free Culture*. New York: The Penguin Press.

Levidow, L. (2002), 'Marketizing higher education: neoliberal strategies and counter-strategies', *The Commoner*, no. 3, [online] www.commoner.org.uk/03levidow.pdf

Lisewski, B. (2004), 'Implementing a learning technology strategy: top-down strategy meets bottom-up culture', *ALT-J*, 12, (2), 175–88.

Lourdel, N., Gondran, N., Laforest, V., Debray, B. and Brodhag, C. (2007), 'Sustainable development cognitive map: a new method of evaluating student understanding', *International Journal of Sustainability in Higher Education*, 8, 2, 170–82.

Lytras, M. D., Naeve, A. and Pouloudi, A. (2005), 'A knowledge management roadmap for e-learning: the way ahead', *International Journal of Distance Education Technologies*, 3, (2), 68–76.

Machlup, F. (1955), 'Some misconceptions concerning academic freedom', *AAUP Bulletin*, 41, 753–84.

Malcolm, J. (2000), 'Joining, invading, reconstructing: participation for a change?', in J. Thompson (ed.), *Stretching the Academy*. Leicester: NIACE, pp. 12–22.

Martinez-Pons, M. (2003), *Continuum Guide to Successful Teaching in Higher Education*. London: Continuum Books.

Marton, F. and Säljö, R. (1997), 'Approaches to learning', in F. Marton, D. Hounsell and N. Entwistle (eds), *The Experience of Learning: Implications for Teaching and Studying in Higher Education* (2nd edn). Edinburgh: Scottish Academic Press, pp. 39–58.

Marx, K. (1993), *Grundrisse: Foundations of the Critique of Political Economy*. Harmondsworth: Penguin Classics.

Maskell, D. and Robinson, I. (2002), *The New Idea of a University*. London: Haven Books.

Maslow, A. (1943), 'A theory of human motivation', *Psychological Review*, 50, 370–96.

Massey, D. (2007), *For Space*. London: Sage.

McGivney, V. (1990), *Education's for Other People: Access to Education for Non-Participant Adults*. Leicester: NIACE.

McLeish, J. (1976), 'The lecture method', in N. Gage (ed.), *The Psychology of Teaching Methods*, 75th Yearbook of the National Society for the Study of Education. University of Chicago Press: Chicago, cited in J. Biggs (2003), *Teaching for Quality Learning at University: What the Student Does* (2nd edn). Maidenhead: SRHE and Open University Press.

McWilliam, E. (2002), 'Against professional development', *Educational Philosophy and Theory*, 34, (3), 289–99.

Menand, L. (1996), 'The limits of academic freedom', in L. Menand (ed.), *The Future of Academic Freedom*. Chicago: University of Chicago Press, pp. 1–20.

Metzger, W. (1987), 'Profession and constitution: two definitions of academic freedom in America', *Texas Law Review*, 66, 1265–322.

Miller, A. (2001), *Einstein and Picasso – Space, Time and the Beauty that Causes Havoc*. New York: Basic Books.

Morrison, D. (2008), 'Pathfinder network projects', [online] elearning.heacademy.ac.uk/weblogs/pathfinder/?p=159

Murphy, M. and Fleming, T. (1998), 'College knowledge: power, policy and the mature student experience at university', paper presented at: Research, Teaching and Learning: Making Connections in the Education of Adults, 28th Annual SCUTREA Conference, Exeter, July 1998.

Murray, P. E. and Murray, S. A. (2007), 'Promoting sustainability values within career-oriented degree programmes: a case study analysis', *International Journal of Sustainability in Higher Education*, 8, 3, 285–300.

National Student Survey [online] www.hefce.ac.uk/learning/nss

NCIHE (National Committee of Inquiry into Higher Education) (1997), *Higher Education in the Learning Society* (The Dearing Report). London: NCIHE.

Neary, M., Lambert, C. and Hanley, C. (2007), *Reinvention Centre Interim Report*. Coventry: Reinvention Centre for Undergraduate Research, Warwick University. [online] www2. warwick.ac.uk/fac/soc/sociology/research/cetl/about/evaluation/reinvention_evaluation_ july_2007.pdf

Nelson, C. and Watt, S. (2003), *Office Hours: Activism and Change in the Academy*. Abingdon and New York: Routledge.

Nelson, J. (1990), 'The significance and rationale for academic freedom', in A. S. Ochoa (ed.), *Academic Freedom to Teach and to Learn: Every Teacher's Issue*, Washington, DC: National Educational Association, pp. 21–30.

Newman, J. H. (1853), *The Idea of a University*. New York: Doubleday.

Noble, D. F. (1998), 'Digital diploma mills: the automation of higher education', *First Monday*, [online] www.firstmonday.org/issues/issue3_1/noble/index.html, 3 (1).

Noyes, A. (2002), 'Learning landscapes', *British Educational Research Journal*, 30, (1), 27–41.

O'Keefe, D. J. (2002), *Persuasion: Theory & Research*. Thousand Oaks, CA: Sage.

O'Reilly, T. (2005), 'What is Web 2.0: design patterns and business models for the next generation of software', O'Reilly Media Inc., [online] www.oreillynet.com/pub/a/oreilly/tim/ news/2005/09/30/what-is-web-20.html

Oakley, F. (1997), 'The elusive academic profession: complexity and change', *Daedalus*, 126, (4), 43–66.

Oblinger, G. and Oblinger, J. (2005), 'Is it age or IT: first steps toward understanding the net generation', in D. G. Oblinger and J. L. Oblinger, (eds), *Educating the Net Generation*. EDUCAUSE E-Book. [online] www.educause.edu/IsItAgeorIT%3AFirstStepsTowardUnders tandingtheNetGeneration/6058

Office of Public Sector Information (1992), *Further and Higher Education Act*. London: Office of Public Sector Information.

Onwueme, I. and Borsari, B. (2007), 'The sustainable asymptogram: a new philosophical framework for policy, outreach and education in sustainability', *International Journal of Sustainability in Higher Education*, 8, (1), 44–52.

Pascarella, E. T. and Terenzini, P. T. (2005), *How College Affects Students* Vol. 2: A Third Decade of Research. San Francisco: Jossey-Bass.

Pawson, R. and Tilley, N. (1997), *Realistic Evaluation*. London: Sage.

Peters, H., Pokorny, H. and Sheibani, A. (1999), 'Fitting in: what place is accorded to the experiential learning mature students bring with them to higher education', paper presented to SCUTREA, 29th Annual Conference, University of Warwick, 6 July.

Petty, R. E. and Cacioppo, J. T. (1981), *Attitudes and Persuasion: Classic and Contemporary Approaches*. Oxford: Westview Press.

Post, R. (2006), 'The structure of academic freedom', in B. Doumani (ed.), *Academic Freedom after September 11*. New York: Zone Books, pp. 61–106.

Pratt, J. (1997), *The Polytechnic Experiment: 1965–1992*. Buckingham: Society for Research into Higher Education and The Open University.

Prensky, M. (2001), 'Digital natives, digital immigrants', *On the Horizon*, 9, (5), NCB University Press, [online] tinyurl.com/ypgvf

Pritchard, R. M. O. (1998), 'Academic freedom and autonomy in the United Kingdom and Germany', *Minerva*, 36, 101–24.

Prosser, M. (2005), 'Why we shouldn't use student surveys of teaching as satisfaction ratings', *The Higher Education Academy*, [online] www.heacademy.ac.uk/research/Interpretingstudentsurveys.doc

Prosser, M. and Trigwell, K. (1999), *Understanding Learning and Teaching. The Experience in Higher Education*. Buckingham: SRHE and Open University Press.

Rabban, D. (1998), 'Can academic freedom survive postmodernism?' *California Law Review*, 86, (6), 1377–89.

Ramsden, P. (1998), *Learning to Lead in Higher Education*. London: Routledge, cited in K. Trigwell and S. Shale (2004), 'Student learning and the scholarship of university teaching', *Studies in Higher Education*, 29, (4), 524–5.

Rancière, J. (1991), *The Ignorant Schoolmaster: Five Lessons in Intellectual Emancipation*. California: Stanford University Press.

Read, B., Archer, L. and Leathwood, C. (2003), 'Challenging cultures? Student conceptions of "belonging" and "isolation" at a post-1992 university', *Studies in Higher Education*, 28, (3), 261–77.

Reay, D., David, M. and Ball, S. (2005), *Degrees of Choice: Social Class, Race and Gender in Higher Education*. Stoke-on-Trent: Trentham.

Reay, D., Crozier, G., Clayton, J., Colliander, L. and Grinstead, J. (2007), ' "Fitting in" or "standing out": working class students in higher education', paper presented to BERA Conference, Institute of Education, September 2007.

Richardson, J. (2005), National Student Survey: Interim Assessment of the 2005 Questionnaire. HEFCE report, [online] www.hefce.ac.uk/pubs/rdreports/2005/rd20_05/

Roberts, C. and Roberts J. (eds) (2007), *Greener by Degrees: Exploring Sustainability Through Higher Education Curricula*. Gloucester: University of Gloucestershire.

Rochford, F. (2003), 'Academic freedom as insubordination: the legalisation of the academy', *Education and the Law*, 15, 249–62.

Rogers, C. (1983), *Freedom to Learn for the 80s* (2nd edn). Columbus, OH: Merrill.

Rorty, R. (1996), 'Does academic freedom have philosophical presuppositions?' in L. Menand (ed.), *The Future of Academic Freedom*. Chicago: University of Chicago Press, pp. 21–42.

Rose, G. (1993), *Feminism and Geography*. Minnesota: University of Minnesota Press.

Rowe, D. (2002), 'Environmental literacy and sustainability as core requirements: success stories and models', in W. Leal Filho (ed.) *Teaching Sustainability at Universities*. Peter Lang: New York.

Rucker, D. D. and Petty, R. E. (2004), 'When resistance is futile: consequences of failed counterarguing for attitude certainty', *Journal of Personality and Social Psychology*, 86, (2), 219–35.

Rudd, T., Colligan, R. and Naik, R. (2006), *Learner Voice: a Handbook from Futurelab*. Bristol: Futurelab. [online] www.futurelab.org.uk/resources/documents/handbooks/learner_voice pdf

Russell, R., Criddle, S. and Ormes, S. (1998), Information Landscapes for a Learning Society UKOLN conference report. [online] www.ariadne.ac.uk/issue16/landscapes/intro.html

Ryan, S. (2001), 'Succeeding despite the odds: a narrative of hurdles obstructing lifelong learning pathways', paper presented at the 31st Annual SCUTREA Conference, University of East London, 3–5 July.

Salmon, G. (2000), *E-moderating: The Key to Teaching and Learning Online* (2nd edn). London: Taylor and Francis.

Salmon, G. (2005), 'Flapping not flying', *ALT-J*, 13, (3), 201–18.

Sanders, C. (2004), 'Casual culture props up academe', *Times Higher Education Supplement*, 1 October. [online] www.timeshighereducation.co.uk/story.asp?storyCode=191546&sectioncode=26

Sanders, C. (2006), 'Students, think twice before you tick us off', *Times Higher Education Supplement*, 10 February.

Sarles, H. (2001), 'A vision: the idea of a university in the present age', *Organization*, 8, (2), 403–15.

Sastry, T. and Bekhradnia, B. (2007), *The Academic Experience of Students in English Universities, Executive Summary*. Oxford: Higher Education Policy Institute. [online] www.hepi.ac.uk/.

Schön, D. (1995), *The Reflective Practitioner: How Professionals Think in Action*. Aldershot: Avebury.

Schuller, T. and Field, J. (2002), 'Social capital, human capital and the learning society', in R. Edwards, N. Miller, N. Small and A. Tait (eds), *Supporting Lifelong Learning* Volume 3, Making Policy Work. London: Routledge, pp. 76–87.

Scott, P. (1995), *The Meanings of Mass Higher Education*. Buckingham: SRHE and Open University Press.

Scott, P. (2005), 'Divergence or convergence? The links between university teaching and research in mass higher education', in R. Barnett (ed.), *Reshaping the University: New Relationships between Research, Scholarship and Teaching*. Maidenhead: McGraw-Hill, pp. 53–66.

Scribner, S. (1985), 'Vygotsky's uses of history', in J. Wertsch (ed.), *Culture, Communication and Cognition: Vygotskian Perspectives*. Cambridge: Cambridge University Press, pp. 119–45.

Scruton, R. (2001), 'The idea of a university', *Salisbury Review*, 20, (1), 4–8.

Scull, A. (2007), 'The fictions of Foucault's scholarship', *Times Literary Supplement*, 5425, 3.

Searle, J. R. (1993), 'Rationality and realism, what is at stake?', *Daedalus*, 122, (4), 55–83.

Seel, N. M. and Dijkstra, S. (eds) (2004), *Curriculum, Plans, and Processes in Instructional Design: International Perspectives*. London: Lawrence Erlbaum Associates.

Serafin, E. (2006), 'Learning landscapes: the use of landscape as a metaphor for the design and implementation of learning systems', paper presented at Association of Learning Technology Conference, Edinburgh, 5–7 September. [online] **www.alt.ac.uk/altc2006**

SFC (Scottish Funding Council) (2006), *Spaces for Learning: A Review of Learning Spaces in Further and Higher Education*. Edinburgh: Scottish Funding Council.

Sharpe, R. (2004), 'How do professionals learn and develop? Implications for staff and educational developers', in D. Baume and P. Kahn (eds), *Enhancing Staff and Educational Development*. London: RoutledgeFalmer, pp. 133–53.

Sharpe, R. and Benfield, G. (2005), 'The student experience of elearning in higher education', *Brookes eJournal of Learning and Teaching*, 1, (3), [online] www.brookes.ac.uk/publications/bejlt/volume1issue3/academic/sharpe_benfield.html.

Shephard, K. (2008), 'Higher education for sustainability: seeking affective learning outcomes', *International Journal of Sustainability in Higher Education*, 9, (1), 87–98.

Shiell, T. C. (2006), 'Three conceptions of academic freedom', in E. Gerstmann and M. J. Streb (eds), *Academic Freedom at the Dawn of a New Century*, Stanford: Stanford University Press, pp. 17–40.

Shils, E. (1995), 'Academic freedom and permanent tenure', *Minerva*, 33, 5–17.

Sipos, Y., Battisti, B. and Grimm, K. (2008), 'Achieving transformative sustainability learning: engaging heads, hands and hearts', *International Journal of Sustainability in Higher Education*, 9, (1), 68–86.

Sjoberg, G. (1998), 'Democracy, science and institutionalized dissent: toward a social justification for academic tenure', *Sociological Perspectives*, 41, 697–721.

Skelton, A. (2005), *Understanding Teaching Excellence in Higher Education: Towards a Critical Approach*. London: Routledge.

Slaughter, S. and Leslie, L. (1997), *Academic Capitalism: Politics, Policies and the Entrepreneurial University*. Baltimore, MD: Johns Hopkins University Press.

Smith, D. (1999), 'The changing idea of a university', *Higher Education Policy Series*, 51, 148–74.

Smith, P. and Rust, C. (2007), 'Students' expectations of a research-based curriculum: results from an online questionnaire survey of first year undergraduates at Oxford Brookes University', *Brookes eJournal of Learning and Teaching*, 2, (2). [online] bejlt.brookes.ac.uk

Snelbecker, G. E. (1999), 'Current progress, historical perspective, and some task for the future of instructional theory', in C. M. Reigeluth (ed.) *Instructional-Design Theories and Models*. London: Lawrence Erlbaum Associates.

St. Laurent, A. M. (2004), *Understanding Open Source and Free Software Licensing*. Sebastopol, CA: O'Reilly Media.

Starik, M., Schaeffer, T. N., Berman, P. and Hazelwood, A. (2002), 'Initial environmental project characterisations of four US universities', *International Journal of Sustainability in Higher Education*, 3, (4), 335–46.

Stuart, M., (2000), 'Beyond rhetoric: reclaiming a radical agenda for active participation in higher education', in J. Thompson (ed.), *Stretching the Academy*. Leicester: NIACE, pp. 23–35.

Sullivan, P. (2007), 'The National Student Survey. Just another hurdle to justify our crust?', *Educational Developments*, 8, (1) 19–21.

Surridge, P. (2006), The National Student Survey 2005: Response and survey methodology. HEFCE Report.

Surridge, P. (2007), The National Student Survey 2006: Findings. HEFCE Report.

Tapper, E. P. and Salter, B. G. (1998), 'The Dearing Report and the maintenance of academic standards. towards a new academic corporatism', *Higher Education Quarterly*, 52, (1), 22–34.

Taylor, R. (2000), 'Concepts of self-directed learning in higher education: reestablishing the democratic tradition', in J. Thompson (ed.), *Stretching the Academy*. Leicester: NIACE, pp. 68–79.

Temple, P. (2007), *Learning Spaces for the 21st Century: A Review of the Literature*. Higher Education Academy.

Terenzini, P. (2005), 'What is learned at university: the U.S. experience', paper presented to the symposium of The Social and Organizational Mediation of University Learning, Cambridge University, 22 September.

Tett, L. (2000), ' "I'm working class and proud of it" – gendered experiences of nontraditional participants in higher education', *Gender and Education*, 12, (2), 183–94.

Thomas, L. (2001), *Widening Participation in Post-compulsory Education*. London: Continuum Books.

Thompson, J. (2000), 'Introduction', in J. Thompson (ed.), *Stretching the Academy*. Leicester: NIACE, pp. 1–11.

Thorens, J. (2006), 'Liberties, freedom and autonomy: a few reflections on academia's estate', *Higher Education Policy*, 19, 87–110.

Thrift, N. (2008), *Non-Representational Theory: Space, Politics, Affect*. London and New York: Routledge.

Tierney, W. (1993), 'Academic Freedom and the Parameters of Knowledge', *Harvard Educational Review*, 63, (2), 143–60.

Tight, M. (2003), *Researching Higher Education*. Maidenhead: Open University Press.

Tosh, D. and Werdmuller, B. (2004), 'Creation of a learning landscape: weblogging and social networking in the context of e-portfolios', [online] eduspaces.net/bwerdmuller/files/61/179/Learning_landscapes.pdf

Traver, A. G. (1997), 'Rewriting history? The Parisian secular masters' apologia of 1254', in P. Denley, *History of Universities* Volume XV. Oxford: Oxford University Press, pp. 9–45.

Trigwell, K. and Shale, S. (2004), 'Student learning and the scholarship of university teaching', *Studies in Higher Education*, 29, (4), 523–36.

Trow, M. and Fulton, O. (1974), 'Research Activity in American Higher Education', *Sociology of Education*, 47, (1), 29–73.

TUC-NUS (2006), All work, low pay: the growth in UK student employment. [online] www.tuc.org.uk/extras/allworklowpay.pdf

Turner, J. (1988), 'The Price of Freedom', in M. Tight (ed.), *Academic Freedom and Responsibility*. Buckingham: SRHE/Open University Press, pp. 104–13.

UNESCO (1997), 'Recommendation concerning the status of higher education teaching personnel', Records of the General Conference, Twenty-ninth Session, 21 October–12 November 1997, Volume 1 Resolutions. Paris: UNESCO, pp. 26–36.

UNESCO (2000), 'Wilhelm Von Humboldt'. *Prospects: The Quarterly Review of Comparative Education*, 23, (3/4), 613–23.

UNESCO (2005), *United Nations Decade of Education for Sustainable Development 2005–2014: Draft International Implementation Scheme*. Paris: UNESCO.

Virno, P. (1996), 'Notes on the "General Intellect"', in S. Makdisi, C. Casarino and R. E. Karl (eds), *Marxism Beyond Marxism*. London: Routledge, pp. 265–72.

Virno, P. and Hardt, M. (1996), *Radical Thought in Italy: A Potential Politics*. Minneapolis: University of Minnesota.

Vygotsky, L. (1962), *Thought and Language*. Cambridge, MA: The MIT Press.

Vygotsky, L. (1978), *Mind in Society: The Development of Higher Psychological Processes*. Cambridge, MA: Harvard University Press.

Warburton, K. (2003), 'Deep learning and education for sustainability', *International Journal of Sustainability in Higher Education*, 4, (1), 44–56.

Warmington, P. (2007), 'Popular press, visible value: how debates on exams and student debt have unmasked the commodity relations of the "learning age"', in A. Green, G. Rikowski and H. Raduntz (eds), *Renewing Dialogues in Marxism and Education: Openings*. Basingstoke: Palgrave Macmillan, pp. 215–28.

Warner, D. and Palfreyman, D. (2001), *The State of Higher Education*. Buckingham: Open University Press.

Warschauer, M., Knobel, M. and Stone, L. (2004), 'Technology and equity in schooling: deconstructing the digital divide', *Educational Policy*, 18, (4), 562–88.

Watson, D. and Taylor, R. (1998), *Lifelong Learning and the University. A Post-Dearing Agenda*. London: Falmer Press.

WCED (World Commission on Environment and Development) (1987), *Our Common Future*. Oxford: Oxford University Press.

West, E. (1963), 'A counterblast to Robbins', STATIST, 1–5. [online] www.ncl.ac.uk/egwest/pdfs/counterblast.pdf

Westera, W. (2004), 'On strategies of educational innovation: between substitution and transformation', *Higher Education*, 47, 501–17.

Whitehead, A. N. and Russell, B. (1973), *Principia Mathematica*. Cambridge: Cambridge University Press.

Wieman, C. (2004), 'Professors who are scholars: bringing the act of discovery to the classroom', paper presented at The Reinvention Center 2nd National Conference, Washington DC, November 2004, [online] www.reinventioncenter.miami.edu/conference_04/wieman/presentation.htm

Wolf, A. (2002), *Does Education Matter? Myths about Education and Economic Growth*. London and New York: Penguin Books.

WPCSUP (Working Party of the Committee of Scottish University Principals) (1992), *Teaching and Learning in an Expanding Higher Education System* (The MacFarlane Report). Edinburgh: SCFC.

Wright, S. (2004), 'Markets, corporations, consumers? New landscapes of higher education', *Learning and Teaching in the Social Sciences*, 2, 71–93.

Yudof, M. G. (1987), 'Three faces of academic freedom', *Loyola Law Review*, 32, 831 58.

Zamorski, B. (2002), 'Research-led teaching and learning in higher education: a case study', *Teaching in Higher Education*, 7, (4), 411–27.

Zuber-Skerritt, O. (1992), *Professional Development in Higher Education*. London: Kogan Page.

Index